THE THREE MOST POPULAR IMMORTALS

LU TUNG PIN

The most popular of the Immortals, he is associated with both medicine and the elixir of life. He has the power over evil spirits through charms. Sick people visit his shrine, and those in danger invoke him to tame evil spirits.

TI KUAI LI

The clown figure who takes the form of a beggar, he uses his power to fight for the rights of the poor and those in need. His popularity rests upon being seen as one of the downtrodden, but he is really more powerful than the strongest oppressor.

CHANG KUO LAU

The bringer of offspring, his image is often found hanging above bridal beds or in the homes of young married couples hoping for children.

Although they do not have the same cult-like following, the five remaining Immortals are equally as fascinating, with unique and distinct personalities. Here, in one re-markable volume are 28 enchanting adventures of the eight Immortals to delight and entertain as they reveal the world of popular Chinese culture.

By the same authors

THREE LIVES
ESSENTIAL TEACHINGS OF ISLAM
ESSENTIAL TEACHINGS OF BUDDHISM
THE CONTEMPORARY I CHING

The
Eight Immortals
of Taoism

Legends and Fables of Popular Taoism
Translated and Edited by
Kwok Man Ho and Joanne O'Brien
Introduction by Martin Palmer

A MERIDIAN BOOK

MERIDIAN
Published by the Penguin Group
Penguin Books USA Inc., 375 Hudson Street, New York, New York 10014, U.S.A.
Penguin Books Ltd, 27 Wrights Lane, London W8 5TZ, England
Penguin Books Australia Ltd, Ringwood, Victoria, Australia
Penguin Books Canada Ltd, 2801 John Street, Markham, Ontario, Canada L3R 1B4
Penguin Books (N.Z.) Ltd, 182-190 Wairau Road, Auckland 10, New Zealand

Penguin Books Ltd, Registered Offices: Harmondsworth, Middlesex, England

Published by Meridian, an imprint of New American Library, a division of
Penguin Books USA Inc.
Originally published in Great Britain by Random Century Group Ltd.

First Meridian Printing, February, 1991
10 9 8 7 6 5 4 3 2

LIBRARY OF CONGRESS CATALOGING-IN-PUBLICATION DATA

The Eight immortals of Taoism : legends and fables of popular Taoism / translated
    and edited by Kwok Man Ho and Joanne O'Brien : introduction by
    Martin Palmer.
        p.   cm.
    ISBN 0-452-01070-5
    1. Pa Hsien (Taoist mythology)   2. Mythology, Taoist.   I. Ho, Peter Kwok
Man.   II. O'Brien, Joanne.
    BL 1923.E54   1990
    299'.514213—dc20   90-22715
                                                                         CIP

Printed in the United States of America

Contents

Introduction

This book is primarily designed to appeal to those who enjoy a good story. The tales of the famous Eight Immortals of China must rank amongst some of the most enjoyable legends of the world. It would be difficult to imagine a more intriguingly idiosyncratic bunch of characters and the fact that they are in part human and in part divine adds to their attractiveness.

Any good story from a different culture, or even from our own, offers more than just a good yarn. These stories were not written by authors or invented by publishers looking for a new market. They represent the age old craft and setting of the story teller — part monk, part fortune teller, part grandfather or grandmother, part temple, part local festival. All these elements go to form the matrix from which these stories have emerged. The process by which some stories survive and become part of the fabric of life while others burn brightly for a short time and then disappear, means that those stories which survive have a staying power which is greater than their content. They touch a nerve, a hope or an aspiration within the listener and speak of the human condition. The stories of the Eight Immortals are no exception. They can be enjoyed purely and simply as wonderful tales. But they can also be used as ways into the complex and fascinating religious and cultural world of popular Chinese thought from where they originally arose, and within which they have survived to this day and will survive for years to come.

So who believes in the Eight Immortals? That is rather like asking who believes in saints. The answer is all sorts of people for all sorts of reasons. Go to any popular Chinese theme garden, the Tiger Balm Gardens of Hong Kong for example, and you will find sculptures of the Eight Immortals in scenes from one or other of their legends. Look on the artifacts shelf in Chinese restaurants in New York, London or Manchester and you will find the eight figures prominent alongside other such folklore figures as Kuan Yin, the goddess of Mercy, and Kuan Ti, the god of War. But the origins of the Eight Immortals and the place where they still command official respect is religious Taoism with its sacred mountains, temples and fascinating philosophies of immortality.

Visit any Taoist temple and you will find the eight symbols of the Immortals arrayed in front of the main temple or in front of the main altar. Usually mounted on spear-like poles, they have the task of warding off evil influences. At certain great festivals these poles, with their symbols, are paraded through the streets to bring good fortune on the area and to keep evil spirits in their place. Figures of the famous Eight will be found carved all around the temple and its precincts, or painted on eaves and walls. Sometimes a shrine to one or other of the Immortals, usually Lu Tung Pin, will be found within the temple compound.

Chinese Buddhist temples also feature the Eight Immortals, though the traditional Taoist symbols for them are not usually found. Instead pictures of the Eight's various exploits will often appear as decoration and frequently one or two of the main characters will have their statues amongst the lesser deities.

Finding the Way

It is necessary to go back to the extraordinary history of religious Taoism to uncover why the Immortals occupy such an all pervasive place in popular Chinese religion, although they are rarely invoked or directly worshipped as a group.

The origins of what we know as Taoism lie far back in the earliest history of Chinese culture. The roots lie in the shamanist background which China shares with large areas of Siberia and Asia. Shamanism, still practiced to this day in parts of China, Japan, Indonesia and, it is believed in Siberia, is the belief in a powerful and all pervasive spirit world which is both interlocked with this world and also set apart. Communication with the spirits is through the medium of a shaman, one who is able to open him or herself to the spiritual forces and so foresee the future, control illness and make prophecies. It is a magical and highly charged world of trances and apparently superhuman feats, such as walking upon burning coals or being pierced with sharp instruments. At its core is a desire to be in tune with, responsive to and, to some degree, in control of the natural forces around you.

Taoism as we know it today is the result of extraordinary transformations to this basic format of shamanism. For Taoism falls into two forms, with apparently little to link them at times. The first form, and the one best known to the West, is philosophical Taoism, known as Tao chia meaning the 'school of the Way'. The other form, which is visible wherever the Chinese live, is Tao chiao meaning 'religion of the Way'. The word 'Tao' which lies at the heart of these two systems means 'way' as in the path or way to truth. It is frequently taken to mean being in harmony with the fundamental natural forces and laws of the cosmos and so following the natural way.

The founder figure of the Tao chia school of Tao is Lao Tzu (see also page 44), a title meaning Old Master. Whether Lao Tzu ever existed as a historical person or not (he is usually set around the period of the fifth century BCE) is a matter of great academic debate. What is not doubted is that the short mystical book attributed to him, known as the *Tao Te Ching*, formed the basis for philosophical and meditational Taoism. In contrast to the public and authoritarian nature of Confucianism, Taoism offered the way of surrender to the ebb and flow of nature as the way to fulfillment. It turned its back on the world of commerce and particularly on the world of the court and statesmanship in favour of the silence and remoteness of meditation in the mountains. Here, away from the hubbub of urban China and the theories of statecraft and family duty of the Confucianists, the Taoist sought reconciliation and oneness with nature. This attitude can be seen clearly in the stories of the Eight Immortals. Several of the Immortals went to remote mountains to practice Taoist meditation and many of the stories of the Immortals feature encounters with wise sages or incarnations of Lao Tzu on mountain sides or in forests. Tao chia produced some of the most beautiful and thought provoking writings on the spiritual quest, such as the *Tao Te Ching* and the *Lieh Tzu*, as well as remarkable writings of sharpness and wit such as the *Chuang Tzu*. However, the classic period of Tao chia lasted only a few hundred years before a new force took over and set the stamp on what was to become mainstream popular Taoism.

In the early second century CE, a remarkable movement of magical Taoism developed in China. Although a number of figures emerged around the same time, the key figure was Chang Tao Ling. He founded a sect or cult which issued charms and talismens to protect the faithful and practised magical healing and spiritual disciplines designed to enhance life. Much of the impetus for this came from the old shamanistic roots, but newer elements of personal salvation were added. Chang's group, known as the Five Bushels group, because they asked for five bushels of rice as payment or membership fees from the faithful, soon became so powerful that they were able to establish, albeit only for a short time, an independent state. In other areas of China similar groups emerged around this period of great political and social unrest, due at least in part to the gradual but inevitable collapse of the Han dynasty which had ruled for over three hundred years from 207 BCE.

Perhaps because of its early aspirations to temporal power, (aspirations which have constantly affected Taoism, giving rise over the centuries to numerous Taoist secret societies intent upon overthrowing the ruling dynasty), Taoism established a vast and complex system of gods, who were given responsibility for every conceivable aspect of human life. Some of these gods come from the deification and anthropomorphosis of shamanistic forces such as the sun, rain, rivers and mountains. Others arise from imperial Chinese posts, such as the district god or the city god who mirror exactly the role of the local prefect or the city mayor. Others are historical figures, who because of the life they have led, are deified, in order to represent either particular interests or to act as moral exemplars.

A devout family would need to pay attention and make suitable offerings of incense to the earth god of the actual land on which they live and run their business, the local god in the neighbourhood temple, the district or city god for the wider area they live in, the gods of literature if they have sons studying, the gods of the various diseases which might affect them, the year god, and so on. Certain gods would also have to be worshipped on special days in each month (these are listed in the Chinese almanac – the *T'ung Shu**). For example, month five (Chinese months do not correspond directly to Western months as the Chinese use a lunar calendar and lunar years are ten to eleven days shorter than solar years) has these special days:

> birthday of the South Star of Longevity; day of sacrifices to the Earth; birthday of the Mother of the Sea Dragon; birthday of one of the gods of the Five Directions; birthday of the City god; birthday of the son of the god Tai-shan; birthday of Kuan Ti, god of War; festival of the day heaven and Earth united and creation began; birthday of the Old Royal Mother, guardian of the peaches of immortality; birthday of Tan-yang Ma; birthday of Hsu-wei Hsien Wang, an immortal (not one of the Eight).

In all this vast array of deities, the Eight Immortals bounce with a vigour and a degree of holy anarchy which is both refreshing and popular. Just as the Buddhist tales of Monkey and his companions combine a good story with humour and certain anarchic elements

---

*Available in an English translation, *T'ung Shu – The Ancient Chinese Almanac*, edited by Martin Palmer, Rider 1986.

while still managing to put across key Buddhist teachings, so the tales of the Eight Immortals combine the same diverse elements and similarly manage to convey, in a popularist way, key Taoist teachings.

We need, however, to return to the strange history of the origins of Taoism in its religious form to fully understand the key role played by the Eight Immortals in popular Chinese culture. Namely, what is an immortal and how do you become one?

The Path to Immortality

Taoism offered something unique in Chinese faith prior to the widespread following of Buddhism. It offered personal salvation and freedom, something the hierarchical and fundamentally worldly creed of Confucius did not offer and indeed even rejected. The salvation Taoism offered differs greatly from that known in the West, for Taoism developed a fascinating theory and series of practices designed to ensure complete physical as well as spiritual immortality. An intriguing theory as to why the physical body mattered so much was put foward by the French sinologist, Henri Maspero. He claimed that it was necessary to retain the physical body otherwise the souls which constitute each person would dissipate at death and the individual identity or make-up of each person would be lost forever. Others see the reason lying in the Chinese belief in three forces or elements of the universe – named Heaven, Earth and Humanity. If only we can continue to exist, then we can partake fully in the cosmic and thus eternal forces. To do this we simply needed to be fully in tune with the forces of Heaven and Earth, and also physically existing as living human beings.

Whatever the reason, a fundamental belief in the importance of immortality has played a very powerful role in Chinese life. References to belief in immortality go back to the third and fourth centuries BCE. One of the cruellest Chinese emperors was Ch'in Shih Huang Ti who ruled the first fully unified China from 221-210 BCE and who is now renowned as the Emperor who built the tomb of the soldiers found at modern day Sian. Whilst being chiefly recalled for his acts of dictatorial terror such as burying Confucianists alive, he is also remembered for having been obsessed with immortality. When he heard tales of the Isles of Immortality, where the necessary ingredients for a pill of immortality could be found, from one of his court magicians, Hsu Fu, he equipped massive fleets to go in search of these islands. One such fleet carried three thousand young people plus artisans of every kind. In the works of Chuang Tzu (written c. 300 BCE) the Emperor read of the chih jen, the 'Realised Man'. This person is able to walk on water, travel the skys and live forever. Ch'in Shih Huang Ti's advisors told him that if he kept out of sight they would be able to make him a 'Realised Man', a suggestion which to modern ears sound likely to have been based upon fears of assassination attempts. In order to comply with this and so gain the chance of immortality, Ch'in Shih Huang Ti ordered his workmen to link twenty square miles of palaces with covered corridors. The scale of this man's obsession with the possibility of actually achieving immortality acts as a very accurate measure of the intensity of the belief in immortality as well as the intensity of the quest.

In order to understand the stories of the Eight Immortals and to enter the world of belief within which they dwell, it is necessary to look more closely at this idea of immortality, and at what it can highlight for us of the fundamental outlook and aspirations of the vast majority of the Chinese for some two to three thousand years.

As we have seen above, immortality in the Chinese context means not just spiritual immortality, but physical as well. Indeed, it is the physical which is the more important of the two. Without the physical, there can be no spiritual. Ancient Chinese religious thought, prior to the arrival of Buddhism, rejected or did not know of the idea of reincarnation. The idea that there was a continous element, the soul or 'atman' which is reborn in a new body after each death, found no place in ancient Chinese thought. For the Chinese, no body meant no soul. Your continuing importance after your death was entirely in relationship to whom you were before your death. The roots of this lie, to some extent, in ancestor worship. Ancestor worship set the seal for many centuries upon the possible notions of the after-life. The body and soul were seen as being the same thing. They were two sides of the same coin and the one without the other was impossible. What is the point one might ask of worshipping your ancestor, of asking him to protect or enhance the fortunes of the family, if he is no longer your grandfather, but has been reborn as, say, a goat! Obviously this was impossible. Your grandfather must remain precisely that – your grandfather.

This was one of the hardest philosophical and popular ideas with which Buddhism had to engage as it began to move into China. For Buddhism sees the soul and the body as completely separate in that the body is but a temporary home for the soul or atman, which continues from life to life until it eventually frees itself from all physical association and needs and disappears or, to use Buddhist terminology, enters Nirvana. The ancient Chinese notion of the body and soul is well captured in a page of the writings of the great Buddhist writer and philosopher Hui-yuan, who lived from 344 CE to 416 CE. In a collection of his writings known as the *Hung Ming Chi*, there is an essay in which he argues against the common Chinese understanding of the body and soul, but in order to do so, he first presents this traditional Taoist viewpoint:

> The endowment of the vital force (ch'i) is confined to a single life. With the termination of that life it melts away again so that there is nothing left but non-being. Thus soul (shen), though a mysterious thing, is a product of the evolutions of the yin and yang; evolving, they produce life, and again evolving, they produce death. With their coalescence there is a beginning and with their dispersion an end. By extending this principle we may know that soul and body evolve together, so that from their origin onward they do not constitute separate sequences. . . . As long as the dwelling [the body] is intact, the vital force remains coalesced so that there is a spirit. Upon the disintegration of that dwelling, the vital force dissipates so that the intelligence is extinguished.*

The logic of this argument, that without the body there can be no soul and vice versa, led to the Chinese notion of immortality. If you want to be immortal, then that means all of you has to become immortal. The body and soul must remain intact in order to gain immortality. And only through immortality could one attain any real continuity of being.

As we saw above, in looking briefly at Maspero's theory (see page 11), humanity is the third part of the triad which sustains and maintains the universe. Heaven and earth, the other parts, we know are everlasting. It is only humanity which is not. But if we are the third leg of the triad, then surely we ought to be capable of becoming everlasting too. The reason why we die, according to the ancient Taoist sages, is because we do not live in harmony with the fundamental ways of the universe, the Way of Nature or the Tao. If we could achieve complete harmony with the Tao, if indeed we could become the Tao, then we would also be everlasting. It was this formula – 'become the Tao by being in harmony with the Tao and live forever' – which launched the Chinese on the quest for immortality, a quest which led along so many diverse and fascinating avenues and created, along the way, the stories of the Eight Immortals.

*Quoted in Fung Yu Lan's *A History of Chinese Philosophy*, vol II, Princetown University Press, 1973.

The August Ones

Like all good Chinese beliefs, tradition places the origins of realising how immortality could be achieved in the dim and distant past. In Chinese terms this means during the era of either the Three August Ones or the Five August Emperors. These mythological beings, possibly based upon some half remembered historical figures, were supposed to have lived and ruled China from around 3000 BCE to 2000 BCE. They are credited with inventing or revealing just about everything from writing to divination, agriculture to money, medicine to hydraulics. For our purposes we need to go back to the figure of the Yellow Emperor, Huang-ti (see also page 44). He was supposed to have reigned from 2696 to 2598 BCE, itself an achievement of longevity! To him are ascribed all the foundation teachings which later became religious Taoism and to some extent, philosophical Taoism. In poplar thought, Hang-ti brought forth the original ideas and Lao Tzu polished them for the new development which started with his own teachings. Thus Taoism is sometimes known in Chinese as Huang-Lao.

The Yellow Emperor has many books attributed to him, such as feng shui (earth magic) manuals and other divination systems. But he is most famous as one of the founder figures of Chinese medicine. Amongst the earliest medical texts is the *Huang Ti Nei Ching Su Wen*, or *The Yellow Emperor's Classic of Internal Medicine*. Composed somewhere between 350 and 280 BCE, it purports to be the details of instructions given to and by the Yellow Emperor concerning all manner of illness and physical aspects of health. For our purposes, its greatest interest lies in the fact that the first chapter is concerned with immortality and longevity as signs of right living. The idea that being in perfect harmony with Tao means the survival of the body and thus the spirit is clearly stated:

I have heard that in ancient times there were the so-called Spiritual Men; they mastered the Universe and controlled Yin and Yang [the two principles in nature]. They breathed the essence of life, they were independent in preserving their spirit, and the muscles and flesh remained unchanged. Therefore they could enjoy a long life, just as there is no end for Heaven and Earth. All this was the result of their life in accordance with Tao, the Right Way.*

The Yellow Emperor's Classic is usually dated from the mid third

*Quoted from *The Yellow Emperor's Classic of Internal Medicine*, translated by Ilza Veith, University of California Press, 1966.

century BCE. It comes, therefore, in the earliest stages of the first rush of material about immortality and health, which was such a feature of the ponderings of the Taoist sages and philosophers. In these ponderings the *Tao Te Ching* of Lao Tzu has played a major role, but not in the way that many in the West imagine. From at least the third century BCE the book was being used as a coded tome of esoteric teachings, magic and the occult, which could provide the key to the Way, which in turn would lead to immortality. Much of this hung initially upon the ideas expressed above, namely that if one lived according to the principles of the Tao then one could aspire to become the Tao and thus escape physical and spiritual demise. However, as the link with the medical treatise of the Yellow Emperor shows, the idea of a purely mental alignment with the Tao resulting automatically in the continued well-being of the physical body, led to concern being focused upon the body itself. From this arose the school of physical and medical Taoism, known sometimes in a rather clinical way as the School of Hygiene.

This aspect of the quest for immortality took two main forms. One was the practice of alchemy, including attempts to find the elusive 'pill of immortality' while the other was the development of esoteric and sexual practices designed to preserve or rejuvinate the body.

The Pill of Immortality

The alchemical quest, which according to Joseph Needham in his monumental *Science and Civilisation in China*, resulted in the Taoists making a series of accidental but highly significant chemical and scientific discoveries, also produced some very strange not to say lethal prescriptions. The quest for immortality by the pill led Taoists and many charlatans to use all sorts of materials. Those creatures which were supposed to live to a great age were highly favoured as ingredients. Cranes, turtles and tortoises, cicadas and butterflies were all credited with living to great ages and were freqently to be found gently cooking in the alchemist's pot. Pine was also favoured as another long living species. But the two most popular ingredients were cinnabar and gold. Cinnabar seems to have earnt its place because of its red colouring. Red is the lucky colour of Taoism and was seen as revitalising the blood supply. Gold achieved its place of honour because it is pure and never rusts or decays. It was therefore seen as being one of the core, fundamental elements of the world – one of the Five Elements of Chinese science along with fire, wood, water and earth. Alchemists believed that if the body could turn to gold or be filled with gold, then the imperishable qualities of gold would manifest themselves within the person's body.

In the minds of certain rulers and alchemists, the pursuit of immortality through the consumption of gold and the pursuit of wealth through the creation of gold by alchemy, seem to have merged into virtually a single quest. The Emperor Wu, known as the Martial Emperor, (reigned 141-87 BCE) is an interesting illustration of this. During his reign he massively expanded China's territory and domination, essentially creating the boundaries of state and influence which were to persist for over two thousand years. His military forces were amongst the largest ever assembled by rulers of the ancient world. This explains one reason for his great interest in alchemy's claim to be able to transmute base metals into gold – paying for vast armies is a costly business. But he also sought for the elixir of life, presumably feeling that he was already doing well, given the length of his reign. He was constantly offered formulas by Taoist adepts, both serious and blatantly fraudulent. As each one failed to produce the desired effects, the alchemists paid for their temerity with their lives. Wu also sent armadas of ships out to find the Isles of Immortality, P'eng-lai, but again, to no avail. It is perhaps a fitting epitaph to the speculative games of the majority of Taoist alchemists that Wu is reported to have said this towards the end of his life, when he saw that they could deliver neither gold nor the Isles of Immortality – 'If we are temperate in our diet and use medicine, we make our illnesses few. That is all we can attain to.'

The Original Breath

Alongside the Taoist alchemists were those who sought immortality through inner purification. This inner purification or strengthening was brought about by a strange mixture of meditational practices and quasi-medical practices. This is probably one of the most truely esoteric areas of Taosim and is also one of the most easily misunderstood. In order to begin to appreciate what lay behind these practices, we need to remember that the quest for immortality saw the body and the soul or spirit as totally interwoven. Thus Taoism could teach skills which developed the spiritual capacities of a person – as is the case in all major faiths – as well as teach semi-medical skills such as retaining the semen. In Taoism, the one without the other simply did not make sense. The body was as essential to immortality as the soul. In this Taoism radically differs from other major Eastern faiths such as Buddhism and Hinduism, in which the body is actually seen as a hinderance or obstacle to the development of the soul, a material prison of the spiritual soul, in fact.

It is important to stress here that the methods which we are about to describe were usually only practised by a few. Taoism, especially in its earlier days was not a mass religion for the path it prescribed was an arduous one to be taken alone. Only late in the second century CE did Taoism begin to develop a dimension popular to the masses. Then, the techniques which we will describe fell into disuse in many areas and more popular and, as some view it, more debased versions, arose.

The most well-known of the Taoist spiritual/physical exercises for achieving immortality are the breathing exercises or techniques. Traditional Chinese medicine believes that it is the breath which causes the body to come to life and the departure of it brings the body to an end. With this, modern Western science can hardly disagree. However, the Chinese identified a number of types of breath which circulated within the body or certain parts of the body. Some were seen as being benevolent, some were malignant and some were neutral but could be affected by disease or spiritual distress elsewhere in the body. Great attention was paid to the regulation of these breaths and vast manuals of breathing techniques were produced. What might surprise us is the aim of some of these techniques. For example, the purpose of the practice known as Embryonic Breathing was to rediscover the nature and origin of the vital breath which first gave life to the foetus in the womb. The question of how a child breathed in the womb greatly intrigued Taoists. They knew it was through the umbilical cord not through the mouth, but what nature of breath is it that first brings the vital force of life to the materials growing in the womb? Are they ever separate? How is life born at conception? The adepts felt that if only they could understand and master the method of the entry of the vital first breath, the embryonic breath, then, they could be born again in their adult body.

In order to do this, a range of breathing exercises were developed. One obvious one was learning to retain the breath. Since the taking in of breath was life giving, the exhaling of breath must be the root of death. If the adept could retain breath, then life would be contained and the vital force kept safe within the body. So techniques were taught whereby the breath was retained for longer and longer periods before finally breathing out. But breath escaping from the mouth or nose was not the only way in which the vital force was lost. There is much made in the various texts of not eating spiced foods nor the 'Five Grains'. One reason for this was that they gave people wind and this meant that part of the vital breath of the body was lost! In later years, from around 600 CE onwards, the idea evolved that each person was born with what came to be known as the Original Breath. This was even given exact measurements – 'three inches inside and three inches outside'. The aim of the techniques now became the sustaining or retention of the Original Breath. It was held that the loss of one inch of the Original Breath took away 30 years of life and conversely the ability to keep each inch increased your lifespan by 30 years. Needless to say, those who never lost any of their Original Breath were already immortal.

From the concern with the breaths came the interest in physical exercises designed to assist the breaths. In many of the texts we are told that the breaths encounter three main areas of resistance. The first of these is below the heart, the second is inside the viscera (especially the intestines) and the third is in the lower Cinnabar Field (just below the stomach). It requires firm discipline and intention to enable the breaths to pass through these areas of resistance, and thus nourish the whole body, and one way of getting the breaths past these obstructive areas is through gymnastic exercises. The basis of the gymnastic dimension of the quest for immortality was a rigorously adhered to formula of exercises, performed at prescribed times, in accordance with strict rules and always facing in the most auspicious direction. Exercise enabled the breath to pass evenly around the body, the forces of yin and yang were balanced and a general sense of well-being was engendered. The time used in exercising the body was also a time for exercising the mind. The adept would use the period for reflecting on Taoist teachings or in preparing himself for a sustained period of intense reading of the Taoist classics. Prayer, invocation and the offering of incense often preceded the respiratory and gymnastic exercises. In a state of heightened awareness brought about by these exercises and techniques, the adept would be better able to understand or read the Taoist masters and thus ensure that the Tao was not just a physical but also a spiritual harmony.

Heaven Falls upon the Earth

Many of the Taoist exercises for immortality are still practised in public to this day. But another physical aspect of the early Taoist quest for immortality was officially suppressed over six hundred years ago, though it has survived in various forms. This was the use of sexual techniques for gaining immortality. It has to be said that like all aspects of Chinese traditional belief, the quest for immortality was an essentially male orientated one. Of the Eight Immortals there is only one woman, and no-one is quite sure how she got there. In the images of the Taoist people of the mountains, the hermits, it is men who are featured not women. Indeed the Chinese character for immortal consists of two other characters joined together – one is the sign for man (not used generically) and the other is the sign for mountain. It is not surprising therefore that most of the sexual techniques for achieving immortality were for the retention of the semen. The semen was believed to be the active force which made the woman fertile. The woman was seen as being like a fallow field waiting for the seeds of life to be sown.

From at least the days of the Han dynasty (207 BCE-220 CE), Taoism produced a stream of books and manuals on sexual practices designed to assist in the goal of immortality. For many hundreds of years such books made up a part of the vast Taoism Canon of Scripture. But by the time of the Ming dynasty (1368-1644 CE) the Canon had been purged of these tomes and their existence virtually denied. Yet at a popular level the practices, often in a debased form, continued.

Essentially, Taoist sexual techniques sought to liberate the soul and body by feeding back into them the very forces which the sexuality of women sought to draw out. Many Taoist writings about women are sexist and, at times, of such insensitivity as to make the modern reader stop short. But we should not fall too quickly into the easy game of condemning earlier ages for attitudes which nearly all society then held. Because the emission of semen was considered one of the surest ways of losing the vital life power, women were to be feared for that reason. They were often refered to as pits into which men fell, as traps full of deadly sharp weapons or as exhilirating rides which led only to the fall and demise of the rider.

It might be thought that the natural response to such feelings of fear about women would be to turn to chastity and abstenance. However, this would run against the natural course of things as determined by the forces of yin and yang, the fusion of the male and female principles. Yin and yang are the pillars of Chinese natural and philosophical wisdom. They are not divine, but simply the two forces which keep the world, the universe, in fact everything, working. They are conflicting forces – male/female, light/dark, fire/water and so forth. They constantly struggle to excel over each other and yet one can never defeat the other. This titanic struggle is what fuels all life and keeps the world, the cosmos, spinning. Because the world is kept going by the interaction of these forces, to withdraw from sexuality would be to deny the very nature of the universe and to place oneself outside the flow of forces which immortality hoped to lead you into. So sexuality had to be encompassed by Taoism – or to be more accurate, by Taoist men.

There is a saying which captures these efforts to come to terms with sexuality. In order to give it a ring of authority it appeals back in time to the semi-historical, semi-mythological Yellow Emperor. The saying goes – 'The Yellow Emperor lay with twelve hundred women and became immortal; common folk have but one wife and destroy their lives. Knowing and not knowing, how could these not produce contrary results? When one knows the procedure the ills deriving from lying with women become few.'

The procedure was how to have and enjoy sexual intercourse without ejaculation. In this setting, the more women you could lie with in one night without ejaculating, the better your chances of immortality. For by summoning up the semen but then feeding it back into your own system to nourish and feed your vital spirit, you were prolonging life. If each ejaculation was seen as taking one year of your life, then the reverse was also true. Thus, the Taoist adept seeking to achieve a life of ten thousand years (Chinese term meaning forever) had, as it were, a formal requirement to engage in approximately that many acts of intercourse! Formal Taoist texts encourage men to engage in dozens of acts of intercourse each night, preferably with a different partner each time.

The texts are also quite detailed about the kind of woman that an adept should chose to lie with. They are always described as 'young' and they should be largely ignorant of Taoist practices and teachings, otherwise they will use them to gain immortality for themselves. Exactly how a woman does this is never satisfactorily explained, but it seems that she could rob a man of his immortality by diverting the life forces from the man into herself.

The main continuing reminders of the esoteric Taoist sexual practices are the strange and sometimes delightful Chinese names for certain styles of sexual action. Based upon the yin yang theory, all such actions are capable of translation into cosmic terms. Thus one has terms such as 'the dragon mounts the deer' or 'the Jade Spear enters the Lute String' or 'Heaven falls upon the Earth'. Nowadays, the sexual practices of Taoism are rarely used. That they brought disrepute upon Taoism is beyond doubt, since the potential for misunderstanding the theory behind such practices led to excesses and thus to official disapproval. Furthermore, the withholding of the semen ran totally contrary to the Confucianist ideal of the family and was always viewed with concern by the official government (except during the few years when certain Emperors made Taoism the official religion). Intellectually, China never accepted the Taoist sexual practices, but emotionally, it found many of them titilating and good subject material for illustrated books of sexual techniques. Yet it was probably the invasion by nomadic peoples, the hordes of the Steppes, which spelt the death knell to such practices being seen as an official part of the Taoist Canon. The Yuan dynasty from 1260-1368 CE was a Mongol one. The Mongols did not have much time for such fancy ideas and seem to have seen such practices as a sign of moral weakness. The official suppression of the Taoist texts on sexual practice seems to date from their time.

There remains one other area of Taoist sexual technique which deserves brief mention. From the fourth to seventh centuries CE certain sexual practices were performed in public and often en masse. We know about them primarily from the writings of one Chen Luan, who converted from Taoism to Buddhism and, like so many converts, then set out to attack his former faith. His book *Taoism Ridiculed* should not therefore be seen as an objective study of Taoism, but it does mention certain aspects of Taoist life in the sixth century CE which we might otherwise not know about. Apparently, such ceremonies took place on nights when the moon was full and were proceeded by fasting. They were designated as ceremonies for deliverance from guilt. Terms such as 'the coiling of the dragon' and 'the playing of the tiger' were used to describe what appears to have been a climax of sexual intercourse in and around the temple between many different partners. The practices seem to have originated or to have taken definite shape under the extraordinary figure of Sun En. Sun En lived towards the end of the fourth century CE and was a famous Taoist master. He is recorded as being only interested in the sexual techniques as a means to immortality and built up quite a following. That this group saw themselves as a public group and not just a group of quiet disciples is shown by the fact that at the start of the fifth century, Sun En led them in an armed revolt designed to establish a Taoist kingdom. This revolt was swiftly crushed.

Before leaving the field of sexual paths to immortality, it is worth making one observation. Whilst the texts are sexist because the society was sexist, they are also very beautiful and graceful in their descriptions of sexuality. There is no suggestion of brutality or of coercion. There is no place here for sadism or masochism. Sexuality was normal, indeed, normative for it reflected the yin yang divide and union of the cosmos. To partake was natural. What Taoism did was to develop a system which took this and found within it a supposed path to immortality.

Taoism for the People

Having now looked in some detail at the more esoteric practices which Taoism developed, we need to return to the ordinary Taoist lay person, seeking to live a mundane but successful life and unable to simply disappear to the mountains to seek immortality. What of him, and to a lesser degree, her? At first Taoism basically ignored such people. The philosophical Taoism of the last four centuries before Christ had little to offer them. It was only with the coming of the popular Taoism movements, the Tao chiao, that lay people began to have a role within Taoism. It is this aspect which has continued to this day. Thus it is virtually impossible to find a 'pure' text of the *Tao Te Ching* in a modern Chinese city such as Hong Kong, but you will find many copies of the *Tao Te Ching* with commentaries by later Tao chiao masters, explaining what Lao Tzu meant by such and such a phrase relating to magic or breathing techniques or charity. Furthermore, you will also find many books which present the more simple exercises and breathing techniques of the masters in modern terms of health and prosperity. However, one of the most popular ways of trying to achieve immortality was by gaining merit. This is an obvious development based upon the success of the Buddhist concept of merit and reward and its appeal to ordinary folk is clear. By undertaking certain practices, certain acts of charity and good deeds, the ordinary person could begin to move themselves up the ladder of life. This is a move away from the idea of self-realisation, as seen in the vital force nuturing exercises of the early Taoists, to the invocation of celestial help achieved by living according to a pattern of moral behaviour.

By seeking to live a good and humble life, longevity if not immortality could be sought. If that was not easily achieved, then there were always the gods of longevity and immortality who could be invoked (as they still are to this day at the major festivals such as Chinese New Year). It is not easy to define the exact role these gods had. There seems to be no real belief that through prayers or offerings to them immortality or even longevity could be achieved, although longevity could certainly be enhanced by invocation of the god of longevity and his image is essential on all books, almanacs or other items which deal with the measuring out of time or one's life. He seems to be more like an amulet for good luck than a divine force who could be drawn into granting you your wish. In the case of the god of immortality, there is even less to say. Perhaps it is sufficient to say that these figures, whilst being around in art and ritual, seem to be essentially representations of an idea rather than divinities who can bring about a certain state and that they reflect the strange matrix of popular Taoist beliefs. It is within this setting that the Eight Immortals find their niche – popular harbingers of the esoteric cult of immortality.

The Eight Immortals

Let us now turn our attention to the Eight Immortals themselves. Some of the Eight seem to be verifiable historical figures, their dates falling around the time of the T'ang dynasty (618-906 CE). In one of the stories of Chang Kuo Lau, we hear of the Empress Wu summoning him to court. The Empress Wu ruled from 684-705 CE. In the case of Lu Tung Pin, we are told that he was born in the year 798 CE at Yung-lo Hsien. In many of the stories as recorded in Chinese, the picture of life given is very much that of the prosperous T'ang dynasty. This has led scholars to place the earliest traditions of the Eight at the end of the T'ang dynasty with the full corpus of tales developing during the Sung dynasty (960-c.1260 CE) and reaching their fullest 'official' form by the time of the Yuan dynasty (1260-1368 CE).

Lu Tung Pin

Lu Tung Pin is the most popular of the Eight Immortals. His statue can be found in most temples in towns and villages and many grottoes are dedicated to him on the sacred mountains of China. He is venerated for two reasons. Firstly, because he is associated with medicine and with the elixir of life. For example, if you are ill but not sure of what to do, then you pay a visit to one of Lu Tung Pin's grottoes or go to his shrine in the temple. There, using the old fortune telling method of a bamboo container filled with numbered sticks, you offer sincere prayers, describe your symptoms and then shake the container. When a stick falls out, you note the number and go to the prescription shop within the temple grounds or at the base of the mountain. Here you report your number and receive a herbal prescription to take to the herbalist. Lu Tung Pin is the doctor of the poor.

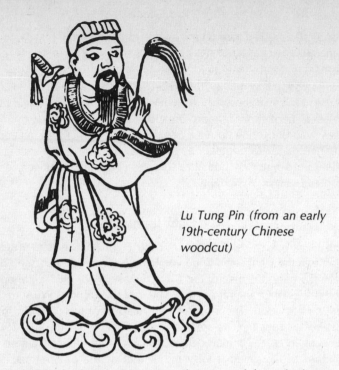

Lu Tung Pin (from an early 19th-century Chinese woodcut)

Lu Tung Pin also has power over evil spirits and through charms. He is usually shown carrying a large sword, his symbol when the Eight are symbolically represented. The sword is known as Chan-yao Kuai, the Devil Slayer. With this sword he is able to capture and tame all evil spirits if he is invoked correctly. Lu Tung Pin's other symbol is a bushy fly whisk, a traditional symbol of one who can fly at will. The field of these Chinese symbols or charms is an enormous one and still immensely popular. The yearly Almanac (the *T'ung Shu*) contains many pages of charms and most Chinese homes will have at least two or three charms pinned to the walls to prevent illness or ward off evil. Lu Tung Pin is seen in the popular imagination as the source of many of the most efficacious charms, although his main source of power is his sword.

In fact, the sword is one of the most potent symbols or charms in Taoism. The other great producer of charms, whose picture appears in almost all yearly almanacs, is the founder of religious Taoism, Chang Tao Ling. His descendents were made into sort of hereditary Taoist 'Popes', although they had none of the power or authority which the West associates with such a title. The Celestial Masters, as they were known, dwelt at the base of Mount T'ien-mu in Kiangsi province until the mid 1930's when they were chased out by the

24

Communists. The greatest possession of the Celestial Masters was an ancient sword, said to destroy or trap devils. This sword was supposed to have been the very one which Chang Tao Ling received from Heaven back in the early second century CE. Thus the use of a sword as a charm against evil spirits is common to both Chang Tao Ling, the Celestial Masters and Lu Tung Pin.

Anyone requesting Lu Tung Pin's help will worship at a temple where appropriate charms can be bought to cover most needs. The medical and magical often merge, for beside many shrines or grottoes of Lu Tung Pin is a container of clear water, usually spring water. This is seen to have magical powers since it is in close proximity to the shrine. For simple ailments, it is enough to drink the water. For certain ailments, a charm is bought, burnt and the ashes added to some of the water, which is then drunk. Finally, for very special ailments, a skilled Taoist Master will make an invisible charm. The Master traces, with his finger, the characters of this charm over a bowl full of water which is then drunk.

Ti Kuai Li

After Lu Tung Pin, the next most popular character is usually Ti Kuai

Ti Kuai Li (from an early 19th-century Chinese woodcut)

Li. He is again associated with medicine and the sign of his iron crutch often hangs outside apothecaries in very traditional areas. However, because of his renowned bad temper and eccentricities, he is not as favoured by worshippers as Lu Tung Pin. He can provide prescriptions, but these are rarely sought by the devout and only if a Taoist priest in a particular area has some link with him. Ti Kuai Li is favoured, however, by professional exorcisists for his magical, medical gourd, his other sign. Ti Kuai Li's popularity seems to rest on his irrascible and unpredictable character. Through no choice of his own, he has the form of a beggar and he uses this to fight for the rights of the poor and those in need. He is very much the clown figure and his popularity rests upon the twin attractions of being seen as one of the downtrodden, who is really more powerful than the strongest, and the clown who is irrascible.

Chang Kuo Lau

Next comes Chang Kuo Lau. He is usually pictured riding his donkey, often riding the poor creature backwards. In his hand is a strange musical instrument consisting of a long bamboo tube with smaller tubes emerging from the top. Pictures of Chang Kuo Lau can be found hanging above bridal beds or in the homes of young

Chang Kuo Lau (from an early 19th-century Chinese woodcut)

Ts'ao Kuo Chiu (from an early 19th-century Chinese woodcut)

couples or couples hoping for children. Chan Kuo Lau is the bringer of offspring, especially boys. For this reason he figures on many calendars produced in the Chinese world and is invoked by worried families. It is difficult to work out why Chang Kuo Lau is given this honour. It is possible that it is actually an ancient case of mistaken identity. There was a very ancient, shamanistic practice of shooting a mulberry wood bow and six wormwood arrows into the air, into the earth and in the four directions to ward off evil at the birth of a son. This practice has now died out, but it is possible that as it died out it was taken over by Chang Kuo Lau. For the phrase 'to bend the bow' used to describe this ceremony sounds the same in Chinese as the phrase 'Master Chang' (chang-kung). Perhaps the tales of Chang and the old phrase have merged over the centuries. Whatever the reason, there he hangs and many hopes hang on him!

The other five Immortals do not have the same personal following or interest amongst the faithful as the first three. They rarely appear by themselves, only usually as part of the famous Eight. Yet their symbols do show certain interesting facets of Taoist belief.

Ts'ao Kuo Chiu

Ts'ao Kuo Chiu is the most unlikely candidate for immortality. He was a member of the imperial court and a dangerous man to cross. His elevation to the rank of immortal seems to have been as an act of caprice by the other seven who wished to fill the eighth cave on their mountain. He was a reformed murderer who seems to have been made an immortal because he looked useful! His symbols are either a pair of castanets or an imperial tablet of recommendation. He seems to have attracted little real devotion down the centuries.

27

Han Hsiang Tzu (from an early 19th-century Chinese woodcut)

Han Hsiang Tzu

Han Hsiang Tzu is much loved. Han Hsiang Tzu's symbol is a beautiful jade flute and he is traditionally seen as the patron of musicians. A great poet and musician, a lover of the solitude and beauty of the mountains, he represents the ideal of a contented person, dwelling in bliss with the basic harmony of the universe and appreciating the beauty of its solitary places. He is, in fact, a true Taoist mountain man.

Han Chung Li

Han Chung Li is a fascinating historical figure who rose high in the imperial service during the Han dynasty (207 BCE-220 CE). Some stories portray him as a General or even Marshal, others as a provincal governor. He is famous for inventing the pill of immortality by alchemy and is a popular figure for those seeking longevity. He either carries a feathery fan which controls the seas or he carries the peach of immortality.

Lan Ts'ai Ho

Lan Ts'ai Ho is the strangest of the group, being at times female, at times male, and at all times very odd. He represents the lunatic, the unbalanced one, a figure recognised in all societies but usually handled better in older societies where it was believed that such

*Han Chung Li (from an early
19th-century Chinese woodcut)*

people were touched by gods or God. He is not worshipped by himself and it is not known why he should hold a basket of flowers, other than for the reasons of enjoying them and seeking to collect all the possible varieties.

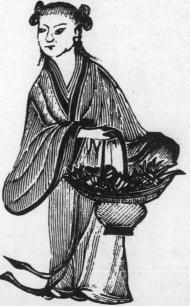

*Lan Ts'ai Ho (from an early
19th-century Chinese
woodcut)*

29

Ho Hsien Ku (from an early 19th-century Chinese woodcut)

Ho Hsien Ku

Finally, there is the one woman in the group (although occasionally Lan Ts'ai Ho is depicted as a woman). This is Ho Hsien Ku who was granted immortality because of her ascetic practices. That there is a woman at all in this group is most surprising, for there is no tradition of female ascetics in Tao chia and the number of senior female practitioners of Tao chiao can be counted on one hand. She is recognised with her lotus flower symbol meaning openness and wisdom. Again, she is not venerated for her own sake.

The Eight Trigrams

For most people the Eight Immortals are simply the subjects of some good stories that are read frequently and consulted from time to time, but they do play one serious role. This is in relationship to the Eight Trigrams and, in particular, to the magical use of the Eight Trigrams for fighting evil.

The Eight Trigrams are a series of three lines, which combine all the variations possible on the theme of either a broken line or a straight line. They form one of the most important sets of symbols in Chinese divination and magic. They are the basis of the *I Ching*, China's most ancient book of divination, and they form the cornerstone of feng shui – geomancy or earth magic. In the *I Ching* they are combined into sets of two trigrams making a total of 64 possible variations. Attached to these are various readings and prognostications. For feng shui, their role is to guard the eight main directions (as in the chart below). Wooden boards with a mirror set in the middle and surrounded by the Eight Trigrams are hung on the fronts of houses or businesses to ward off evil. The second page of the Almanac (*T'ung Shu*) always carries a feng shui compass with the Eight Trigram directions marked upon it. Feng shui is the art by which the Chinese divine where to build and how high to build in order to be in harmony with the natural forces of yin and yang and thus ultimately with the Tao.

Each of the Eight Immortals is associated with a certain Eight Trigram direction. In certain cases this is based upon their characters. Thus, Ho Hsien Ku, as a woman represents yin – the female. This is associated with the south-west and the trigram which represents yin (three broken lines) is placed there. Ti Kuai Li, because of his hot temper, is situated in the south, while the calmer and most elderly of the Eight, Chang Kuo Lau, is placed in the north. Han Chung Li, with his sea stirring or controlling fan, is placed on the eastern side where

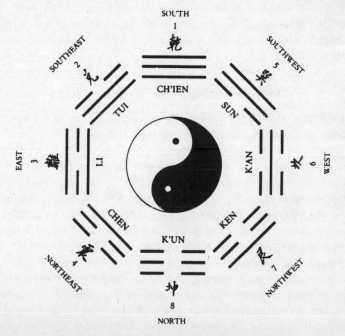

The Eight Trigrams and the Eight Directions

the ocean meets China. Lu Tung Pin, controller of the forces of evil and the unknown, is on the west, traditionally the dwelling place of mysterious and magical forces due to the vastness of the mountains and deserts which lie in that direction. Han Hsiang Tzu defends the south-east, while the last two, Lan Ts'ai Ho and Ts'ao Kuo Chiu, guard the north-west and north-east respectively.

The Eight Immortals and their directions along the Eight Trigrams are invoked in one of the most powerful forms of magic that Taoism has. This is the famed *Pa-chen T'u* – the Battle Chart of the Eight Trigrams, which is used to combat disturbances brought about by a black Taoist master. It is credited to one of the most outstanding but mysterious figures in Chinese magic and divination, Chu-Ko. He is supposed to have lived during the Three Kingdoms period (221-265 CE), though in fact the earliest references to him occur in the T'ang dynasty (618-906 CE), making him a contempory of the Eight Immortals. He is credited with being the founder of the main school of magical Taoism, the Pei-chi or Pole Star school. Although rarely used today, the *Pa-chen T'u* is still held in highest respect as one of the most powerful ways of controlling the spirit forces and calling them down to aid the fight for good. In it, we encounter the old face of the shamanist and his associates, though now bedecked with Taoist immortals, trigrams and other forms of more established Chinese religion. It is this world which we now need to explore more fully.

The Folk Setting of the Eight Immortals

In the tales of the Eight Immortals, we can find many of the key elements of religious Taoism. Taoism has rarely been the official religion of China. Occasional Emperors declared in favour of Taoism over Buddhism, but rarely, if at all, was the official state 'creed' of Confucianism ignored. If this happened, it was usually the very short-lived whim of a profligate Emperor who did not survive long. The official creed was Confucianism. Everything else was judged by its worthiness in relationship to Confucian values. Buddhism was opposed from its earliest dates of entry into China (during the first century CE), because it encouraged monks and nuns. Monks and nuns, by their very vocation, choose to leave their families, not to have children and are unable to support their parents. This was considered unfavourable since it ran contrary to all basic Confucian ideas. Although Taoism advocated the sage and the mountain man, it did not present such a threat. Many of its greatest sages were married and there were so few philosophical, sagely hermits, that they did not present a serious challenge to the supremacy of the family. Moreover, Taoism was Chinese, therefore within the fold, whilst Buddhism came from outside and so was naturally suspect.

The other major difference between Buddhism and Taoism is that Taoism is primarily a folk religion, practised by the peasants and artisans. Officials and scholars might be interested in its alchemy or in the more philosophical concepts which it raised. They might practice Tai Chi Ch'uan, the exercise movements and martial arts which arose from the disciplines developed to aid the search for immortality, but few would be likely to make these personal interests into a show of public support.

The world we encounter in the stories of religious Taoism, and in particular in the stories of the Eight Immortals, is the folk, peasant, working-class world of China. Through these tales we can experience life as it was lived by the vast majority of the Chinese people. Their story is rarely told. The bulk of Chinese literature was written by the literati and for the literati. To hear so clearly the voice of the oppressed, downtrodden masses of China is indeed a privilege. To hear it through such thoroughly enjoyable tales is a double privilege.

So what was the world like for ordinary Chinese people at the time these stories came to be written down, or achieved their current status? While rooted in T'ang traditions, the period they most accurately reflect is that of the Ming Dynasty and the Ch'ing Dynasty – that is to say from 1368 to 1911. In fact, although enormous forces have torn across the face of China since 1911, there is much in contemporary Chinese peasant life that has echoes in the world depicted by the stories of the Eight Immortals.

The world revealed in these stories is a very hard one. The heroes and heroines are often cruelly treated and at the bottom end of the social scale. Frequently they are right at the bottom of the social scale – they are beggars. Begging in China was almost akin to a profession. It was highly organised and most areas would have a beggar king. He was responsible for making sure that the beggars' underground network of petty crime and scrounging worked smoothly. This meant allocating areas for begging to certain beggars or groups of beggars, dealing with disputes within the 'fraternity', maintaining working relationships with the local judges and officials and occasionally assisting in the hunting down of real villains who had committed murder, massive fraud or some other serious crime.

The beggars' 'guilds' were basically a way the poorest of the poor tried to regulate the many factors which made their lives so difficult. On occasion, the beggars would rise up against really corrupt officials, like a vanguard of the poor, and exact revenge. These were never serious attempts at rebellion, but rather, spontaneous outbursts of righteous indignation against the abuse of power by the powerful. This is why beggars are such popular figures in the Eight Immortals' stories. They represent both the sadness of the lowest of the low, plus the threat of retribution against the gross abuse of power. The story of the punishment of K'uang Tzu Lien gives us a very clear picture of this world. The Immortal Ti Kuai Li, who already looks like a deformed beggar, goes to the feast of K'uang Tzu Lien, a rich merchant. K'uang is celebrating his sixtieth birthday. Normally, Chinese people do not celebrate birthdays. Instead, when New Year comes, they simply count themselves one year older. However, the sixtieth birthday is different. The Chinese calendar works on a cycle of sixty years. At the end of sixty years it starts again. Thus, a sixtieth birthday is a real occasion for celebration. At such a celebration it would be normal for the host to offer food for the poor. This would be usually an act of Buddhist piety, for to do so means a better rebirth in the next life. By the Ming period, Taoism had also caught on to this idea, and promised an easier time in Hell if you did acts of mercy while on earth.

In this instance, K'uang does not offer the poor any food. Indeed he goes further. He uses up good rice to level the road for his wealthy guests. He is therefore doubly guilty and must expect retribution. This Ti Kuai Li duly gives him, but only after K'uang has further dug his own pit of damnation by beating the beggar to death.

It is not just beggars however who 'star' in these stories. A whole range of ordinary folk also feature in them. The small shopkeeper is one of these characters. China has always been a country of small traders and shops. Every town would offer a wide range of goods and through the excellent networks of roads and canals, goods travelled widely through China. The merchant class reflected a wide social range, from the great import/export merchants with their fleets of ships and strings of horses, down to the little local shopkeeper struggling to make a living. One such shop and shopkeeping family appears in the story of *The Flower Basket Epiphany* (see page 142). Lan Ts'ai Ho visits a local village and here meets the distraught family of a flowershop keeper. In this story we get a particularly fine picture of life at the rougher end of Chinese society. The family shop has been destroyed by thugs during the night and the family faces ruin. But of greater immediate concern is the fact that the attack has been carried out on the orders of the local landowner. He wishes to take the daughter of the shopkeeper as his concubine, but she is not willing to go. Indeed, she has just married another stock-in-trade figure of the Immortals stories, the impoverished but honest student.

Landowners are on the whole not a good thing in these stories. They are almost always depicted as money grubbing, vicious and overbearing, which was often the case, and one form of oppression, much resented, was the taking of daughters by local officials and landowners. The institution of concubinage was one with long roots in Chinese society. The idea of having a first wife, a second wife and so on, was the respectable form of this. But taking a concubine was often little more than having an official sex slave and servant rolled into one. Chinese literature is full of references to landowners, money lenders or local petty officials using their power over a family in order to abduct a loved daughter. Usually, there was no recourse to justice for the family. The daughter was simply lost to them. The hardship and suffering of these women has been romanticised by the West, which is perpetually intrigued by Eastern sexual mores. But you only have to read stories like *The Flower Basket Epiphany* to see what the ordinary people of China felt about such goings on.

Another figure in this story that we need to look at is the honest but impoverished student. In theory, China's examination system meant that anyone who was bright enough could rise to great fame and fortune. Each year, examinations were held lasting three days. During this time, students were quite literally locked away in tiny cells and given essay topics. The best of each year would then proceed to the next level, until eventually they arrived at the most senior exams. To come top in these, was to ensure a prosperous future through security on the ladder of officialdom.

In theory, this system of examinations should have ensured that anyone with the right skills could succeed. The reality was usually very different. The exams were entirely concerned with regurgitating passages from the Chinese Classics, the great Confucian texts. These had to be used to answer any question, for it was held that all wisdom was to be found within them. The time and effort necessary for a student to learn the Five Classics and Four Books was immense. Twenty years of almost continuous study was not unusual. Few if any ordinary folk could afford to indulge their sons in such study. It was left to the wealthy and official classes to sustain this system, though occasionally someone of lowly origins would break into it. In some areas of China today, you can still see a scholar's tower on the edge of a village or small town. It would have been built by the village or town elders to provide a haven for any budding scholars from their community. Here, children who showed promise at an early age would be sent to study hard. The strain and stress placed upon these children was enormous. The hopes of the whole village or town were on their shoulders, for if they were successful, then they would be expected to shower their home village or town with great favours.

While many students aspired to success in the Imperial exams, few achieved it. Thus the countryside of China was fairly full of impoverished students. Their poverty came about by various means. They might have come from a small village, where it had been decided that enough money had been spent on their studies to no apparent end. Therefore they would be cut off suddenly, but have no practical skills by which to make a living. Or they might be the scion of a great family, which had placed high hopes on their son only to have them disappointed. Again, the disgrace of failure led many such students to wander off and seek oblivion in areas where their family was not known. Finally, there were those students who valued true learning and found none in the rigid system of the official exams and the Classics. Such students would continue their pursuit of knowledge for its own sake. But there would be little money in such a career.

It is significant that students do not often appear in the stories of the Eight Immortals, for they were really a little out of the class of the audience for whom the stories were created. When students do appear, it is to add a certain desperate dignity to an already touching story. Virtually none of the average listeners to these stories would expect to meet such a person, except perhaps in their local schoolmaster.

The Imperial Government

Officials of the Imperial Government were also frequently figures of oppression in the lives of most peasants and workers. The hazards of living in an area with a corrupt judge or official are often illustrated in the Eight Immortals stories. For instance, the corrupt judge in *How Chang Kuo Lau Obtained a Donkey* (see page 122), is a typical example. Easily bought, he has no interest in truth, only in power and money. The results of his abuse of power are pain and suffering for the poor and innocent and there is no recourse against such a person. Another example, only too well-known from Chinese history, is the corruption and crime created by the four brothers of the Queen in *Tsao Kuo Chin Repents His Sins* (see page 128). The greatest fear of the ordinary person in China was of corruption in the highest places, for then there was no hope at all. Once the Emperor or his family went 'bad', then the Empire was in for a very rough time.

A story which illustrates this very well is that of a good and honest official called Ch'u Yuen. He cared deeply for the welfare of the people in his area and always tried to act compassionately and justly. But he had the great misfortune of living at a time when the Emperor was corrupt and surrounded by greedy courtiers. The Emperor used up money as though it were rice! He never had enough for his wants and so taxes were increased time and time again. Life was very hard indeed for the ordinary people of China, and Ch'u Yuen's heart bled for them.

One day, the Emperor passed yet another tax. Ch'u Yuen knew that this tax would spell death from starvation for many of his people. He knew he had to protest. So he wrote a special letter to the Emperor telling him of all the sufferings of the people. This letter, however, was simply laughed at by the Emperor. When Ch'u Yuen heard this he was despondent. As an honourable man, there was only one protest left to him. He walked to the top of the cliff overlooking the lake near the town where he lived. Then he cast himself off from the cliff top and plunged into the lake. Suicide was the only protest he had left to make.

When the townspeople saw their beloved Ch'u Yuen plummeting from the rocks into the water, a great cry of grief went up. Instantly, people took to their boats and raced out into the lake to try and rescue him. Soon the race became even more desperate, for out of the depths of the waters rose the evil water dragons. Snarling and hissing, they headed for the dead body of Ch'u Yuen. Against them raced the devoted townsfolk. The dragons began to overtake the rowers. Then one lad had a bright idea. Most boats had pots of cooked rice in them to feed the fisherman. Grabbing a handful of the wet rice, the lad squeezed it into a ball and threw it into the lake. One dragon dived off after it. Within a few moments, others on the boats were throwing balls of rice into the water and the dragons were diverted. With a final effort, the heroic rowers reached the still body of Ch'u Yuen. They lifted him into the main boat and rowed back to the shore.

When news of Ch'u Yuen's suicide reached the Emperor, along with a letter explaining why he was going to kill himself, the Emperor was shaken to his core. He went into deep mourning, putting far away from him the luxuries which had ruined his country. Within a few days, he had repented of his evil ways and executed his corrupt courtiers. From then on the people of China were justly ruled by the reformed Emperor.

Now, each year the Dragon Boat Festival, is held to commemorate the boat race to rescue Ch'u Yuen's body and this victory of good over evil. It is a very popular folk festival, but was never particularly celebrated by the ruling class!

In the Eight Immortals story, *Ts'ao Kuo Chin Repents His Sins*, there is an example of the just and wise magistrate, Pao Kung. He pursues the quest for justice fearlessly, even when it means judging the Queen's brothers. The integrity with which he works is a good example of the very best in Chinese administration. While much of the bureaucracy of China was indolent, corrupt or just simply absent, the system did throw up men of tremendous integrity and honesty who helped redeem it. Again, the just magistrate who seeks truth and is no respecter of rank, is a figure much loved in Chinese literature. In such figures, the oppressed of China could see some hope for justice, but in reality much of life simply involved surviving amidst the ebb and flow of forces greater than themselves.

Spirits of the Land

It is time now to turn from the 'real' world of the Chinese poor to the 'magical' world they also inhabited. I have deliberately put these words in parenthesis because the distinction is one we might feel justified in making, given our current beliefs. But it is not a distinction which the ordinary Chinese people of the Ming and Ch'ing dynasties would have made (or one which many Chinese living now would make). To them the spirit world was as real as the physical world, at times more real. So let us now explore something of this other dimension of 'reality', as experienced by the audience at which the Eight Immortal stories were originally directed.

We have already looked at the basic religious and philosophical building blocks of Taoist belief. What we have not covered is how all of this expressed itself in everyday life. The Eight Immortals stories are full of assumptions about the spirit world and its forces and the impact they have on people's everyday lives.

One example of the very real overlap between the physical and spiritual world is the religious geography of China. We have noted earlier the links between Taoism, immortals and mountains, to the extent that the Chinese character for immortal is a combination between the character for man and the character for mountain. When the character for mountain is romanised, it is spelt as 'shan'. So, if in the stories you encounter something called, for instance, Hua Shan, you know you are dealing with a mountain.

The mountains of China have always been seen as special places. Some of the stories of the Eight Immortals are about how certain mountains came to have the shapes they have or how particular rock outcrops took on the features they have. In the story of *One Hundred Birds In The Mountain* (see page 133), we learn how the various peaks of Huang Shan took on the appearance of different birds. In any part of China you will find stories which explain the local geographical features. In Hong Kong for instance, there is Amah rock. This rock looks like a woman with a child strapped to her back, looking out to sea. You can imagine the sort of tale which goes to explain Amah rock.

China has a very extensive set of sacred mountains, both real and imaginary. On the real side there are the classic Nine Sacred Mountains. These are divided between the Taoists and the Buddhists. The Taoists, as befits the indigenous faith, have five of the nine. The Buddhists, obviously realising that sacred mountains were necessary for religious street credibility, have managed four! These mountains are very special places. Even in the periods of the worse excesses of the Cultural Revolution, pilgrims still made their way to these holy mountains. To make a pilgrimage and to climb to the peak, visiting each and every shrine is believed to bestow great merit and blessing on the pilgrim. Under the more relaxed current regime, pilgrimages have grown immensely.

It is on these sacred mountains and on some of the other, lesser, holy mountains, that many of the more 'spiritual' adventures of the Immortals take place. The three most important of these are T'ai Shan, Hua Shan and from the lesser mountains, Huang Shan. By looking briefly at these three mountains we can see something of the fusion or interaction between physical geography and divine geography.

Of all the sacred mountains of China, T'ai Shan is the most important. It is the home of the Grand Emperor of the Eastern Peak, who is believed to be the most senior god on earth, appointed by the Jade Emperor (see page 43). It is this god, the Grand Emperor, who decides the length of days of human lives and who passes the dead on to the underworld for judgement. An inscription in one of the temples on T'ai Shan spells out the powers of this deity:

*The Grand Emperor of
the Eastern Peak (from an
early 19th-century
Chinese woodcut)*

To all beings he brings life.
His power presides over the workings of life.

It has long been the tradition that Emperors would pay a visit to T'ai
Shan to receive the blessing of their spiritual equal on earth. With
glee, the story is told of the visit of the first real Emperor of China, the
terrible Ch'in Shih Huang-ti (c.225 BCE). Having bloodily wiped out
the other small kingdoms by the force of his formidable army, Ch'in
Shih Huang-ti began a very brutal reign. He hoped to establish a
dynasty which would last for centuries. In fact, it collapsed within a
few years of his death, so hated was he and his kin.

The story goes that Ch'in Shih Huang-ti came on a solemn pilgrimage to the holy mountain of T'ai Shan. With a vast retinue and the
most wonderful gifts, the Emperor began the long climb up the
mountain. What had begun as a sunny day, soon changed. Dark
storm clouds gathered and strong winds sprang up. Before the procession had even reached the half-way point, the rain was lashing
down and the gifts were being blown away by the unusually strong
winds. The Emperor had to beat an undignified retreat. Needless to
say, this was taken to show that the Grand Emperor was far from
pleased with his earthly counterpart.

The buildings and monuments on T'ai Shan are designed in such a way as to enhance the stunning natural beauty of the place. Solitude is still possible if you turn aside from the main pilgrimage path and seek peace in the folds of the mountain. This aspect of the recluse is often portrayed in the Immortals stories, and the Eight Immortals were very much at home on T'ai Shan. T'ai Shan is also the place where Lao Tzu liked to come, disguised, so as to test the worthiness of his followers. For T'ai Shan is a Taoist mountain – it is the mainspring of the Taoist sacred geography of China and, as such, it is of great interest. As we have noted earlier, Taoism very rarely became the 'official' court religion. This position was largely reserved for Confucianism and, at times, Buddhism. Yet, the Taoism of the land, as represented in the sacred mountains, was very much a part of the cosmology of the court and the Imperial way of life. The five Taoist mountains are seen to form a sacred framework for the geography of ancient China. This geography was both a real one and a spiritual one, in that the five mountains (East, West, North, South and Centre) marked the boundaries of ancient China. Beyond these boundaries lay strange lands and oceans.

The second mountain to occur with some regularity in the Eight Immortals stories is Hua Shan. This is the Western Mountain or Flower Mountain. It is of course the setting for *The Flower Basket Epiphany* story (see page 142). The mountain seems to have had a very special role as a mountain of thanksgiving and of birth, be it of a dynasty or of a child. Legend tells us that the earliest rulers of China, who had gained their power by battle, came to give thanks on this torturous and dangerous mountain track. Stories tell of T'ang the Victorious, who founded the Shang dynasty coming to Hua Shan to offer thanks. Likewise, Wu Wang, founder of the Chou dynasty, came to give thanks for his victory. These are ancient sites.

The fertility role of Hua Shan is shown in *The Flower Basket Epiphany* story with its theme of prodigious production of the finest blooms, capable of becoming beautiful women. It is also interesting to note that Hua Shan even crops up in one of the greatest of Buddhist stories, where kings worship Hua Shan and are then able to have children – the story of Kuan Yin, the goddess of Mercy.

The mountain also has its own store of Lao Tzu legends. Towards the summit there lies the temple of Lao Tzu, in front of which stands a vast furnace in which Lao Tzu was reputed to have made his pill of immortality. If you come on the right night, you might catch sight of Lao Tzu and be rewarded by a taste of the pill of immortality. If this is not possible, then try the special mushrooms which grow on the mountain, for these are also said to grant you immortality.

The Yellow Mountain (Huang Shan) is not one of the five sacred mountains. It owes its holy nature to the array of extraordinary rock formations and the fact that if offers or offered a place of solitude and beauty beside the great Yangtze River. It is also linked in some legends with that strange figure, the Yellow Emperor (see page 44).

The significance of these sacred mountains has to be set within the Chinese understanding of the land itself. Unlike the West, the Chinese have always seen the land as full of forces which control not only the land but all that dwell on it. One of the main sciences of Taoism is geomancy, known in Chinese as feng shui (wind-water). Essentially, geomancy reads the landscape like a book. It detects the forces of yin and yang that lie within the land. It detects the places where the spirits dwell and where powerful forces gather. In the light of all these insights, it then seeks to help people build, farm and plant in accordance with the pattern of the land, both physical and spiritual. Hence, the role of sacred mountains in Chinese thought. The mountains are seen as guardians of the country and as special focuses of spiritual power. But all land is seen like that. Every traditional Chinese home or workplace will have its shrine to the earth god of that particular piece of land. This is still true today. In many of the Chinese restaurants of Europe or America or Australia, if you descend to the basement, you will pass a little shrine of a red and black painted board with joss sticks. This is for the earth god and is by way of an apology and request for the use of the land. On a larger scale, each district, each town, has its own local deity who is responsible for all life in that area. No part of the land or waters of China is without its deity and together they constitute in popular Chinese thought, an administration as formidable and yet as corruptable as any human counterpart.

One of the best examples of all this is the kitchen god. Here the two worlds of the material and the spiritual lie side by side. You will find the kitchen god in any traditional home. He will usually take the form of a piece of paper on which he is sometimes depicted as a god, while at other times as an inscription of invocation. He hangs beside the family stove (sometimes thereby earning himself the name of the stove god) and watches what goes on. As we all know, the kitchen is a place where many secrets are told and arguments held. The kitchen god is therefore perfectly placed to find out all the very best and worst aspects of the family. At the end of each year, on the twenty-third day of the twelfth month, the kitchen god ascends to heaven. This is usually done by burning the paper image or invocation. He reports to the Jade Emperor (see page 43) and the deeds of the family are duly noted for judgement at death, or punishment/reward in this life.

The kitchen god is therefore like a paid informer. Indeed, he is treated as such, but he is also treated with a certain degree of contempt. For instance, when it comes to the twenty-third day of the twelfth month, the day he ascends to heaven to report, many people will smear honey on the lips of the kitchen god before sending him to heaven. This is to ensure that he says only sweet things about the family. Just as he is the paid informer of the Heavenly Court, so he is also the bringer of the blessings or curses of the Heavenly Court. When he is reinstalled early in the New Year, he brings the basic fortune of the family for that year. He is therefore welcomed with much ceremony and good things to eat are placed before him.

The Jade Emperor's Court

The Heavenly Court plays a major role in many of the stories of the Eight Immortals and formed the background against which much peasant life in China was played out.

It is ruled by a very odd character called the Jade Emperor. Although he is the king of the gods in name, and is given the epithet of the most magical and valuable of Chinese jewels, he is in fact a very weak character. To a certain degree he is the classic fall guy of Chinese mythology. While he has at his command the hosts of heaven, in the form of ferocious soldiers, mighty heavenly generals and so forth, he is often unable to enforce his will. Indeed many of the classics of Chinese literature and mythology, such as *Monkey*, are tales of the Jade Emperor and his Court being outwitted. The *Monkey* story is a classic of this genre. It is based upon a true life journey made in the period 629-640 CE by the Buddhist monk, Hiuen Tsiang. He travelled to India in order to bring back certain Buddhist scriptures which introduced the wider Mahayana branch of Buddhism to China. In *Monkey*, the monk is joined by a weird and wonderful collection of fallen characters who are redeemed – but only just – by joining the monk on his very eventful journey. The chief hero of the story is the Monkey King, who has very successfully defied Heaven, the Court, Lao Tzu and the Jade Emperor himself. Now, while the story is at points very scurrilous about Taoists, being essentially a tale of popular Buddhism, it is mirrored by many similar stories from the Taoist folk side. Witness the first story in this collection, *The Jade Emperor's Birthday* (see page 56). So we have a very odd figure at the head of the Heavenly Court, one who ought to be feared but who is actually mocked.

But although the Jade Emperor is often a figure of fun, he is also capable of instilling fear. The natural elements are his domain and he does have some nasty forces he can unleash against those who oppose or upset him. In the stories about Pai Shih (see pages 64, 68 and 70), we see these forces at work. Using natural forces such as lightning and the brutal soldiers of his guard, the Jade Emperor is able to crush the powers of young Pai Shih. But notice that Pai Shih, far from becoming humble and obedient to the will of heaven, sets out to get his revenge and is only defeated in the end by a trick. In a sense, precisely because Chinese beliefs about the spiritual heirarchy are founded upon the Imperial earthly model, they evoke the same mixture of fundamental contempt and admiration, with an edge of fear or caution.

The Yellow Emperor, Kuan Yin and Lao Tzu

While the Jade Emperor is in theory in charge of heaven, there are in fact three other characters who play a much more powerful role, even if two of them are sometimes mocked. These are the Yellow Emperor, Kuan Yin and Lao Tzu.

Let us take the Yellow Emperor first. He is actually credited with being the father of nearly all human knowledge! For instance, he is always linked with medicine, because one of the most famous of all Chinese medical tomes is called *The Yellow Emperor's Classic of Internal Medicine*. He is the original wise man of Chinese legend and a figure of stability and order in an often unstable world. This comes across very powerfully in the story *A Hundred Birds in the Mountain* (see page 133). A semi-historical figure, the Yellow Emperor combines the role of shaman with sage and ruler. He is very powerful and rarely, if ever, is he mocked or tricked in Chinese legend. To do so would be to mock the earthly institute of Emperor.

The second character is Kuan Yin. Kuan Yin is a Buddhist figure, being a bodhisattva, meaning one who could become a Buddha and thus escape the cycle of life, but who chooses instead to stay behind to help others in their struggle to escape rebirth. She is the most popular religious figure in China and has a place in people's hearts which is second to none. Yet because she is a Buddhist, the Eight Immortals stories, with their roots in Taoism, do have some fun with her. This comes out in a gentle way in the story *A Matchmaker for Kuan Yin* (see page 82). Otherwise Kuan Yin is often the figure who comes to people's rescue and gets them out of impossible or awkward situations. She is known as the goddess of compassion or mercy and it is in that guise that she often makes an appearance in Chinese stories. She frequently has to rescue the Jade Emperor from problems he has created for himself.

The third figure we have already met in certain guises and that is Lao Tzu, the founder of the Tao chia school of Taoism (see page 9). Yet he does not escape a certain ridicule. In the Eight Immortals stories he often appears as the wise guide who keeps his real identity

The Chinese Celestial Hierarchy (from an early 19th-century Chinese woodcut)

hidden to test the devotee. Yet he also is pictured at times in Buddhist folklore as a bumbling fool, who is easily outwitted by anyone determined enough. However, in the Eight Immortals stories, he is without doubt a hero figure and has the edge over his nominal lord, the Jade Emperor.

Gods of Earth and Water

Under the rule of the Jade Emperor comes not just the heavenly court but also the gods and goddesses who dwell on the earth or in the waters. These seem to lead a life which is rather like that of a country judge in relationship to the Imperial court. Figures such as the earth god or the tree gods appear, but the most interesting of all, and the ones who are featured most in Eight Immortals stories, are the sea dragons or water dragons. These are powerful forces and not to be played with lightly. The sea or water dragons fall into two main types – the four great sea dragons who rule over the four oceans of Chinese mythological cosmology and their local representatives in each major sea, lake and river.

The four great sea dragons are violent, destructive, proud and overbearing. They seem at times to constitute a force almost apart from the rest of the spiritual world. They are usually pictured as either hostile to humanity or, at the least, very suspicious of humanity. These great dragons have their own sumptuous palaces beneath the waves. Many tales tell of the beauties and riches of these palaces and of the strange sights awaiting any visitor. Here are squadrons of crab soldiers, shark troops, lobster guards and so forth. Here are beautiful sea women and gracious courtiers drawn from the more elegant and delicate of the sea creatures. Something of the diversity and authority of a sea dragon's court is given in the story of *The Jade Emperor's Birthday* (see page 56). The legendary beauty of the sea dragons' daughters is most movingly captured in the sad story of *The Dragon Girl and the Immortal Flute* (see page 139). This story encapsulates the great divide which is believed to exist between the world of the sea dragons and the world of humans.

The second type of sea dragon is more eclectic. He is the guardian of treasure. Usually living alone, he will use any means in his power to protect his treasure. Brushes with such sea dragons are not as serious as those with the rulers of seas, the great sea dragons, but they do often have epic qualities to them. These dragons are also very avaricious and constantly wish to add to their treasure.

The Courts of Hell

If the Heavenly Court is given a mixture of respect and distain, the Courts of Hell are given great respect and yet are viewed as essentially corrupt. Taoism, like Chinese popular Buddhism, has one of the most extensively developed pictures of hell known to humanity. It makes the Christian picture look positively amateur. Taoism having come first, has ten Courts of Hell. Buddhism, not to be outdone, has eighteen Courts of Hell.

The power of the Courts of Hell and their respective judges is great. When your time has come, you must obey their command to attend. The Judges of Hell are known collectively as the Yama. Often referred to as kings, they rule over the fate of all souls and are themselves ruled over by the Judge or King of the first hell. He, in turn, is under the direct rule of the Grand Emperor of the Eastern Peak and the Jade Emperor. In days gone by, the first judge of hell was Yama himself, but he proved to be too kindly, letting sinners off too lightly. So he was deposed and while his title became the collective title, he was demoted to the fifth hell. It is to him that penitents pray for help. The ruler of the first hell is now Ch'in-kuang wang. He judges the soul in its full wickedness. It is in his court that you face the terrible ordeal of the Terrace of Mirrors of the Wicked. Here you look into a mirror and see all those whom you have harmed in any way. Interestingly, this does not just mean human beings, but any animal or creature who has suffered for your sake.

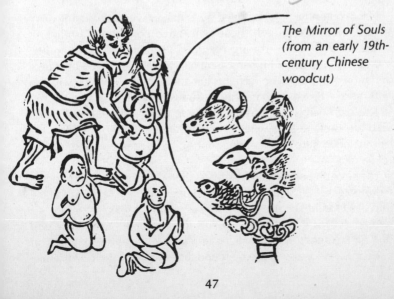

The Mirror of Souls (from an early 19th-century Chinese woodcut)

Let us now look at the other hells, which tell us a great deal about the structure of values in popular Chinese folk life. The second hell is ruled by Ch'u-chiang wang (wang by the way means 'king'). Here those who have acted as go-betweens in a marriage and have been corrupt or dishonest in some way are judged and punished. No one would dream of marrying unless the marriage had been professionally arranged, but the trust which was placed in the professional marriage fixers was often betrayed. Here such people get their come-uppance. In a society where divorce was impossible for all sorts of reasons, a bad marriage was a curse for life especially for the poor. Here also doctors who are frauds or who failed to heal or charged too much are punished, as well as those who have deliberately caused pain to animals.

The third hell is ruled by Sung-ti wang who punishes unfaithful underlings and women who fail to abide by the filial laws. The filial laws, laid down by Confucianism, were very strict. The patterns of authority and hierarchy allowed for no deviation. The wife has to obey the husband and to respect and obey his parents above her own. To break this law was considered a terrible crime. This is captured in the story of *The Bamboo Shoot That Grows Upside Down* (see page 120).

The fourth hell is ruled by Wu-kuan wang and here are judged the rich who never gave to the poor – frequent figures in the Eight Immortals stories. Here also are punished all swindlers and tricksters, the curse of decent working people who see their savings taken by fraud.

Next comes the fifth hell ruled by Yama, as we have already mentioned. Here are judged those who have committed a religious crime – such as destroying religious artifacts or blaspheming, murderers (not just of humans – animals are also avenged by Yama) and monks or nuns who have broken their vows. Here you will also find those who have committed sexual sins, and all prostitutes.

The sixth hell is ruled by Pien-ch'eng wang who punishes those who are profane in language, behaviour or attitude. Amongst the sins included here are dumping rubbish beside temples and making false coins!

The seventh hell is ruled by no less than the Grand Emperor of the Eastern Peak, T'ai Shan. This position refers to the role he has as the lord of all life and death. Here come those who break into tombs – a terrible sin for it destroys the work of the family to placate and honour the ancestors who might then take revenge (see page 49 on ancestors). Here also are to be found those who sell their own family

Judged in Hell (from an early 19th-century Chinese woodcut)

into slavery, especially the women of the family. The story of *The Flower Basket Epiphany* (see page 142) shows with what revulsion such a loss of a daughter causes in ordinary society.

The eighth hell is ruled by P'ing-teng wang who has special horrors in store for those who have been guilty of failing in filial loyalty.

The ninth hell is ruled by Tu-shih wang. This is the most feared hell for from here the only escape is to be returned to earth as a ghost or malevolent spirit. This hell is for those who commit suicide for no honourable reason. Abortionists and those who abuse the written word by producing pornography are also judged here. This is the most terrible hell.

The last hell is ruled by Chuan-lu wang – the king who rules over rebirth. He receives the souls from the other nine hells, after they have been through their terrible punishments. He then determines in what form they will be reborn and sends them out to their next life.

Reincarnation and Ancestor Worship

The idea of rebirth, as given in the last and tenth hell, is an odd one. Most people think of Chinese religion as being involved with ancestor worship. But if your ancestor is reincarnated, how can he or she remain an ancestor? If great grandfather is now living happily as a tortoise, how can he respond to the devout prayers of his family for wealth, health and fertility?

The answer to this is not easy! Essentially Chinese folk religion, of the sort which spawned the Ten Hells of Taoism, is a mixture of religious ideas and messages. There is for instance a very strange relationship between the living and the dead in Chinese traditional belief. The ancestors are certainly to be feared and revered. At all great Chinese festivals, worship of the ancestors is a major part and two major festivals are largely concerned with ancestors. Yet the ancestors are also dependent on the living to get them out of trouble. At Chinese funerals and at festivals where ancestor worship takes place, paper money made out to the Bank of Hell, mock gold and silver bars and models of everyday items such as credit cards, cars and televisions are burnt. It is believed that these then pass to the afterlife where the ancestors can use them to buy their way to a more comfortable position in hell. The original idea was that by such virtuous action your ancestor would intervene on your behalf and you would be guaranteed a better position in the afterlife and be there for a shorter time before being reincarnated. As we discussed earlier, the concept of achieving immortality was a yet higher level of this. Even today, there is still this strong idea that your ancestors can help you, or, to put it another way, if you do not care for your ancestors, they will hinder you.

So ancestor worship is important, but it is worth noting that while a mighty or great figure from your clan history may be remembered and venerated for centuries, normal family veneration lasts only a few generations. Folk religion does not set a timescale on the duration of each soul in hell, but after a certain lapse of time it is usually assumed that an ancestor has reached the stage of reincarnation and therefore ceased to be your ancestor. Thus worship of that ancestor also stops.

The idea of reincarnation was given its main expression in Chinese thought through the writings and teachings of the Buddhists. Buddhism has as a central tenet the concept of reincarnation, of being a prisoner of the wheel of suffering, which brings constant rebirth until you are able to escape the wheel. Buddhism, as mentioned earlier, has always had to compete with Taoism for the attention, funds and devotion of the ordinary Chinese people. Thus Buddhism has eighteen hells as against the Taoist ten. It also has a much clearer system of merit points, by which each action carries with it a clear moral value. These points are added up and count towards your next reincarnation.

However, the fusion of Taoist and Buddhist ideas with certain Confucian principles regarding life after death is typical of Chinese folk religion. One of the most important books on birth rituals amongst ordinary Chinese people is a tome called *The Three Lives*. This book tells you what life you lived before this one, roughly what sort of life you will lead during this life and what you will be in your next incarnation. It is a glorious mixture of Taoist, Buddhist and Confucian deities, practices, values and beliefs. To try to unweave these strands inevitably leads to disappointment, for Chinese folk religion's vitality is that it has woven these very disparate systems into a workable, malleable tapestry.

Changing the Future

Let us now leave the land of the dead for the land of fate and magic. The stories of the Eight Immortals are full of all sorts of magic – but much of this is of the sort that any 'superhero' might do, such as displaying superhuman strength or changing from one guise to another, and so forth. This is the type which so appealed to the downtrodden peasants and workers. However, there is also another form of magic and it is tied in most cases to fate and fortune telling. As we have seen, life for the ordinary Chinese person was tough and unfulfilling. The poor could see the life of ease of the rich and yet could see no apparent reason why one group should be so well-off and another not. The supposed openness of the state examination system meant that it was, in theory, possible to pass from being a member of the underclass to being a member of the privileged class. The merchant structure of China also opened the doors to wealth for those who could find a market to make their own. Furthermore, there were always old grand families in decline or families who had squandered their inherited wealth, to serve as an example that good fortune could also decline into bad fortune.

In such an environment, much more fluid than say feudal Britain, the question of fate and fortune was, and still is, of burning interest. In the West, despite the influence of Christianity in its more Roman Catholic forms, we have tended to equate fate with fatalism. This Greek concept of fate is still very strong in our culture. Thus if we are fated to bring trial and tribulation, even death, upon our own kin, no manner of attempts to avoid this will avail. In the end, we will always fulfil our fate. While mainstream Christianity has taught free will, doctrines such as the Calvinistic ideas of predestination have fed this equation of fatalism with fate.

In Chinese thought we encounter a very different understanding of fate, and it is of great importance to understand what the difference is, for it colours much of Chinese society and behaviour. The Chinese concept of fate is captured in the Chinese word *ming*. This has the sense that while certain things in life are fixed, such as birth, growth, decline and death, who your parents are and whether you are a boy or girl, other aspects are not fixed. It is up to each person to make the best of what they are given (in effect the 'fixed' parts of fate). This still means that they have to take account of forces greater than themselves, but they are at least, to some degree, in charge of their own destiny. The series of stories about Pai Shih (see pages 64, 68 and 70) shows this very clearly.

Imagine if the Pai Shih stories had been told by an ancient Greek storyteller. Then we would have been told that Pai Shih's fate was to suffer at the hands of the heavenly generals and to fail to achieve revenge through the power of a goddess and so on. We would have had to watch prophecies come true despite Pai Shih and his mother's attempts to thwart them. In this setting, the false promise of the Emperor would take on a tragic quality, leading Pai Shih into the inevitable sequence of events which lead to his trials and tribulations. Instead, we have a reverse storytelling procedure. At any given time, Pai Shih is quite capable of achieving his goals and it is just bad luck, poor judgement or downright trickery which stops him. The story is quite open to development in any direction and is not telling an inevitable tale, but exploring the vagaries of human choice and option.

This sense of one's destiny being in one's own hands is central to the Eight Immortals stories. It is the basis upon which the stories are built, in that it is often the kindness of a particular action that brings people the inestimable benefit of the blessing of the Immortals and thus changes their fate. The action is almost always depicted as a spontaneous one, arising from the essential nature of the person. A good example of this is found in the story *P'eng Cho and the Eight Immortals* (see page 148).

Turning to Magic

We have mentioned earlier the power of charms and magic within folk religion, especially within the religious Taoism as established by Chang Tao Ling (see also page 9). Chang Tao Ling is considered, after Lao Tzu himself, to be the most powerful caster of spells in Chinese religion. In the 1930's, when the Communists drove out Chang's descendent from the holy mountain he lived on, they found an incredible sight. There, in row after row of bottles, jars and pots, stretching back over centuries, stood 'demons'. These demons has been captured by Chang and his descendants, the so-called Taoist 'Popes', using charms which went back to Chang Tao Ling himself. In the Almanac, published every year in the Chinese world, you can see Chang Tao Ling seated above household charms for the prevention of illness, financial disaster and marital disharmony. In his hand rests the sword he was given by heaven to capture the demons and which still resides with the present Taoist 'Pope' in Taiwan.

The power of paper charms in Chinese popular belief is enormous and all pervasive and this is reflected in the Eight Immortals stories. The kitchen god, as we have already mentioned, is usually represented by his image on a paper sheet in order to enable him to be burnt at the end of the old year. By burning the paper, the spirit of the kitchen god is sent to heaven (see page 42). The hanging of red paper scrolls, one either side of the main door, is always associated with good luck. Many Chinese shops, businesses or restaurants have

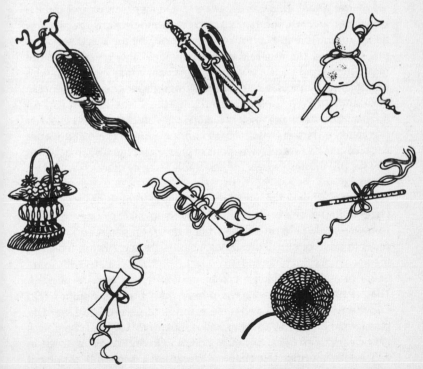

The Symbols of the Eight Immortals (from a 20th-century Chinese drawing)

these and no major new project would be undertaken without such auspicious action. These scrolls are often mirrored in traditional homes and premises by door gods, one on each side of a door. These are to guard against evil forces seeking entrance, while the scrolls themselves are there to attract fortune.

It must be remembered that the world of the traditional Chinese is one filled with evil spirits and forces who have to be guarded against. Chinese belief with its strong sense of two powerful forces (yin and yang) at work in the world, sees such evil forces as being as powerful as the forces of good, although it is always assumed that good, or perhaps more accurately order, will prevail. Thus, simple measures of self-defense against evil forces will work. Many traditional Chinese houses in villages, will have a small, low wall built a few feet in front of the main door into the home. This is the 'devil wall' and is designed to prevent devils rushing into the house. The two gods on the door are then there to scare away any that get past the wall.

In *How Chang Kuo Lau Obtained a Donkey* (see page 122), we encounter a very important instance of a paper charm. A piece of paper cut to resemble a donkey is produced by the blacksmith and then from this charm a real donkey emerges. This is very powerful magic indeed and it is not without significance that the person who performs such magic is a blacksmith. This indicates that this story is a very ancient one, possibly predating the Eight Immortals and adapted later. In many ancient cultures, the blacksmith was a feared and revered person. His ability to transform ore into metal, to work with fire and to produce weapons of great power was seen as a sign that he was in some way a magician and possibly in touch with dark forces.

But such powerful magic is not the normal, run-of-the-mill stuff of charms. Paper charms are usually given to protect or to cure. If someone is ill, a charm will be written down on paper and burnt in order to drive out the illness. Most charms are actually modelled on the ancient format of an Imperial Edict. The charm opens with some figure of authority giving a command that they are to be obeyed. These figures of authority have to have power over the spirit world and the two most favoured are Lao Tzu and Chang Tao Ling. The transformation of Lao Tzu the philosopher into Lao Tzu the god is very clearly seen here. It is quite common to find books in Chinese which take the different chapters of the great Taoist philosophical classic, the *Tao Te Ching*, and interpret them as charms, spells and incantations for everything from impotency to winning at cards.

Introduction

Having gained the authority of some great power, the charm continues, in Imperial language, to instruct the lesser deities, stars on duty, constellations and other assorted forces of the Chinese spirit world, to deal with the particular grievance. The belief is that illness or bad luck is part of a pattern of misbehaviour which needs to be controlled, much in the same way as crime or revolt or simply improper behaviour has to be disciplined by a government or country.

Enough has been said of Taoism and its cultural and historical setting. It is now time to turn to the actual Eight Immortals stories, stories of wit and charm that can tell us more about China's past and her folk culture than any further explanation can.

The Jade Emperor's Birthday

Many years ago, on the eighth day of the ninth month, the Eight Immortals were rowing a boat across Tung T'ing lake. Their small boat bobbed gently in the lake's warm waters as the Eight Immortals drank, sang and played 'guess fingers'. After a pleasant and relaxing day they contentedly watched the sunset which bathed the lake and the geese coming into land in the golden colours of evening. Unexpectedly, the sound of drums and flutes rose from the bottom of the lake and the unruffled surface of the lake was broken. Up from the water rose chariots decorated in colourful flags followed by a battalion of valiant soldiers dressed in red tunics. The soldiers were so busy bustling around and giving orders that they failed to notice the Eight Immortals watching them. Once the soldiers and their retinue had broken the water's surface they continued their journey up to heaven. Anxious to discover what was happening, the Immortals hastily rowed their boat to the nearest shore and summoned Ch'eng Huang, the guardian god of cities. Ch'eng Huang appeared promptly before the Eight Immortals and bowed down low before them.

'What can I do for you?' he inquired.

Lu Tung Pin pointed at the lake and then up to heaven. 'Why are they so busy in the Dragon's palace and why is the Dragon King sending so many soldiers up to heaven?' he asked Ch'eng Huang.

'Oh, don't you know?' replied the city guardian with surprise. 'My dear Immortals, tomorrow is the ninth day of the ninth month, the Jade Emperor's birthday. It is the duty of every god, spirit and immortal to prepare a birthday tribute for the Jade Emperor. If he likes your present he will promote you to a higher rank of god. The Dragon King has spent months preparing for this day and you have only seen a small selection of his gifts being carried to heaven.'

'What nonsense is this,' retorted Ti Kuai Li. 'Why should an immortal pay tribute so that he can be raised to the rank of god? I refuse to flatter the Jade Emperor.'

'Hold on. Please calm down, my great Immortal,' replied Ch'eng Huang. 'I understand what you are trying to say but it is only an entertainment. Why don't you swallow your pride and pay him tribute.'

The Jade Emperor (from a mid 19th-century Chinese woodcut)

'I am not giving a gift,' said Ti Kuai Li adamantly. 'Why should I give the Jade Emperor money when he does nothing for me.'

Ch'eng Huang began to tire of Ti Kuai Li's obstinacy. 'Everybody has a superior whom they should obey. An immortal should obey the Jade Emperor. Even a ghost has to obey the Judge of Hell. It is even possible to trick the Jade Emperor into giving you a title. Although the Monkey King already has seventy-two magic powers,

57

he has been able to trick the Jade Emperor and has been given the title "Holy One".'

'He is only a monkey,' retorted Lu Tung Pin derisively. 'How can you compare a monkey with the Eight Immortals. We like to live a simple life. We do not want wealth or luxuries so there is no point in flattering the Jade Emperor.'

'You may be right in theory,' replied Ch'eng Hang. 'In fact I used to think the same as you but I paid a high price. I had to work for two hundred years to receive my position and now, no matter how hard I work, the Jade Emperor will not offer me another promotion. Many people look down on me and ridicule me. You must remember that the rich and famous have many friends but the poor have few who want to help them. You must know that the immortals are divided into many ranks, some are highly respected and others have very little prestige. If you anger the Jade Emperor he will demote all of you to wild immortals.'

The Eight Immortals mulled over Ch'eng Huang's words for several minutes. Perhaps he was right. The Eight Immortals had worked amongst the poor and the sick for hundreds of years and, although they didn't seek profit or praise, they had never received any recognition from the Jade Emperor. Finally the Eight Immortals decided to follow Ch'eng Hang's advice and offer tribute to the Jade Emperor. Not only would they please the Jade Emperor, but this was also a good opportunity to enjoy an abundant array of free food and drink.

By the time the Eight Immortals arrived at the Jade Emperor's palace the party was in full swing. Colourful lanterns and flowers decorated the golden palace walls and the floor vibrated with the sound of lively music; clear sweet songs of the sea princesses filled the air. The Eight Immortals lined up behind the other immortals and gods before the Jade Emperor's throne. Eventually it was their turn to present their tributes. Chang Kuo Lau stepped forward and offered the Jade Emperor a night cap made of donkey's tail hair and Han Chung Li presented a carved bamboo pen rest. Although the gifts had been made by skilled craftsmen, the Jade Emperor was not impressed, in fact he didn't even offer a smile of gratitude. Lan Ts'ai Ho then took a lotus from his flower basket, but the Jade Emperor was not pleased by its colour or its fragrance and promptly ground it underfoot. Ti Kuai Li presented a porcelain bedpan which he thought would make a perfect gift since the Emperor was growing old. But this was the final straw, the Emperor was so insulted he summoned his guards.

'Take these evil, miserly immortals out of my palace,' he commanded. 'Demote them to lower class immortals and immediately enter them in our registration book.'

The Eight Immortals were extremely annoyed by the time they returned to earth. Ti Kuai Li shook his fist at heaven and scolded the Jade Emperor for being a fool and a rogue and the other Immortals started complaining too. Eventually Ti Kuai Li quietened them down.

'What we need is action not words,' he proclaimed. 'The Jade Emperor has no right to bully the weak and respect the strong. We must teach him a lesson. If the Monkey King managed to cheat him so can we. Lan Ts'ai Ho, please lend me a lotus flower from your basket. I want to use it to steal priceless gifts from heaven.'

Ti Kuai Li held the lotus flower in one arm and jumped on to a cloud which rose straight to the Jade Emperor's palace. A long queue of immortals and gods stretched from the palace reception hall to the golden entrance arch, so Ti Kuai Li put the lotus flower on his head to conceal his identity. He stealthily made his way to the baskets of tributes which had been piled up behind the Emperor's throne. He hastily selected the best gifts he could find and rushed back to join the other Immortals on earth.

'This time the Jade Emperor will invite us to drink with him at his birthday party,' he told the other Immortals with delight. Ti Kuai Li drew out six priceless gifts – a jade unicorn, a jade horse, a diamond ox, a gold tiger, an ivory dragon and a silver lion. The other Immortals were duly impressed but they were two gifts short. Ti Kuao Li was willing to go back to the palace and steal another two gifts but Lu Tung Pin stopped him.

'It's too late to go back to heaven and furthermore you may be caught. Leave this to me. I will find two presents on earth.'

Lu Tung Pin stooped down, parted the grass and caught a handful of fireflies. He held them up to the others, saying proudly, 'The Jade Emperor has never left heaven, therefore, he must never have seen a firefly. If I tell him that this is an illuminated pearl he will have to believe me.'

The other Immortals clapped their hands with delight at this suggestion. Then Lan Ts'ai Ho had an idea. He climbed to the nearest willow tree and carefully collected three autumn cicadas which he put in his flower basket. Without wasting any more time the Eight Immortals set out to heaven. The queue of gods and immortals had disappeared but the palace was still festooned with lanterns, lamps, and flowers and sounds of laughter and music drifted from the inner rooms of the palace. The Eight Immortals swaggered up to the Jade

Emperor who was still sitting on his throne in the middle of the reception hall.

'Wild immortals, how dare you come back to the palace again,' he thundered.

Han Chung Li stepped forward and took a bow before he spoke reverently to the Jade Emperor. 'Your majesty, when we came to celebrate your birthday earlier this evening we failed to bring expensive gifts with us. Please forgive us and accept these priceless gifts from the palace of the human emperor.'

The Immortals presented the stolen gifts one by one to the delighted Emperor. But the Emperor was not completely satisfied with the six gifts and demanded another two. Lu Tung Pin stepped forward and placed the fireflies on the footstool before the throne. As he did so he recited the following words:

'A light wind blows through the jade palace door,
there are no candles or moon to light the palace,
a thousand fireflies dance in the night,
they light up the mountain,
they light up the palace,
they light up the water.'

'Excellent, a perfect birthday present,' congratulated the Jade Emperor. 'Now what about you Lan Ts'ai Ho. What do you have as a present?'

Lan Ts'ai Ho took the three cicadas from a concealed pocket in his robe and gently squeezed them with his fingertips. The cicadas started to sing and once again the Jade Emperor laughed delightedly.

'What a wonderful present! What is the name of this priceless gift?'

'Your majesty, they are called long singing cicadas and are considered to be priceless in the human world,' replied Ti Kuai Li respectfully.

The Jade Emperor stood up from his throne and picked up his gifts one by one, examining them from every angle. Finally he turned to the Eight Immortals and, with an appreciative smile, he gestured to a side table laden with food and drink. The Jade Emperor then summoned his secretary and asked him to inscribe the Immortals' new title in his registration book. Although the Eight Immortals were now officially called the 'Eight Holy Immortals of Heaven's Palace', they never used their title. They only wanted to make a fool of the Jade Emperor and they had succeeded in doing so.

The Grottoes of Chung Ling

Chung Ling mountain in Kweilin is riddled with grottoes, many of which lead into one another. They are tunnelled so deep into the mountain that it is easy to become lost for weeks on end. There is a legend that tells how these grottoes were formed.

Wang Mu, the Jade Emperor's mother decided to build a palace on the banks of the Li River. She was far too delicate to carry the work out herself so she put the T'ai Pin Chin star in charge of its construction. After receiving orders, T'ai Pin Chin summoned the strongest gods in heaven. When they had assembled before him he revealed his ambitious plan.

'Wang Mu has ordered me to build a palace on the banks of the Li River, but the view from the palace is so boring she will be disappointed each time she looks out of the palace windows. I want you to create the most beautiful view in the world using as many mountains as you like.'

The gods were excited by this challenge and before long they had laid mountains of all shapes and sizes around the banks of the Li River. The view was so stunning and the air so pleasant that it attracted hundreds of mountain, earth and river gods and the Eight Immortals made it their favourite resting place.

When the other gods in heaven discovered the theft of so many mountains to decorate the view around the Li River, they were furious. They immediately blamed the Eight Immortals. 'Why should they have the best view in the world leaving the other gods with little more than mud heaps? If the Eight Immortals are allowed to steal, why shouldn't we steal too?' And so, in the dead of night, an army of gods descended to the Li River. They laboured throughout the night and before the first light of dawn, they managed to steal nearly every peak in the area between Li Yu mountain and Yang Shuo's Dragon Head mountain leaving behind scraggy hills and mounds of mud.

By the time the mountain and earth gods woke up their homes had been devastated. They ran panic stricken to Wang Mu to report the violation of their homes. The gods pushed and shoved each other in their eagerness to report the damage and hundreds of agitated voices tried to speak at the same time.

When Wang Mu finally discovered what had happened, she stormed around heaven berating every god and immortal who crossed her path. When she finally calmed down, she had decided on a new plan. The strongest gods in heaven were once again summoned to court.

'I want you to borrow one of the Sea Dragon King's precious pearls,' commanded the Queen. 'Take this pearl and place it under Chung Ling mountain, so that when the other mountains begin to grow their roots will be secured, through the power of this pearl, to the earth for eternity. Not even the Jade Emperor himself will be able to steal those mountains.'

The strong gods carried out her orders and slowly but surely the mountains began to grow again.

One hot summer the Eight Immortals decided to spend their holidays at the Li river. On their first evening they sat on the river bank drinking wine and chatting. Suddenly, the calming sounds of evening were broken by a cry of surprise from Lu Tung Pin.

'Look at the glow coming from Chung Ling,' he shouted excitedly. The others all turned to see what he was talking about and sure enough a pale, eerie glow radiated from the mountain.

'It's a precious pearl,' they cried in unison. And, without any need to discuss the matter further, they jumped to their feet forgetting everything else in their haste to find the pearl.

It was almost dark by the time the Eight Immortals reached the mountain, but nothing short of an earthquake could stop their search. They spread out across the mountain and searched it thoroughly from top to bottom. Not even a rabbit burrow or a cracked stone remained untouched, but the pearl could not be found. By the following morning they sat exhausted but undefeated on the grassy lower slopes of Ching Ling. Each Immortal sat deep in thought until Ti Kuai Li cried out triumphantly, 'If it isn't on the mountain, it's in the mountain. Quick there is no time to waste. We have to find a way of opening the mountain.'

Each Immortal used his or her own special magic power. Ti Kuai Li summoned a scorching fire from his gourd to melt the rock, Lu Tung Pin slashed through the mud and stone with his sword, Ho Hsien Ku turned her lotus flower into a powerful digging tool and Chang Kuo Lau's donkey burrowed deep into the earth. All of them summoned every type of magic they knew. Some drilled into the mountain from the top, others from the middle and others from the bottom. They drilled so fiercely that they met each other in the middle of the mountain. Once they had collided with one another, they just started drilling in fresh directions. They burrowed, chiselled and dug the mountain till it was almost hollow, but they didn't discover the precious pearl. It is still somewhere in Ching Ling mountain. Neither did they refill the passages which is why Ching Ling is riddled with so many deep and dark grottoes.

Pai Shih's Drama

The Old Man's Prophecy

Lu Tung Pin and the other Immortals regularly met at the hermitage on T'ai Shan mountain to discuss Taoist teachings and to meditate.

One autumn Lu Tung Pin caught a glimpse of an unknown woman meditating outside one of the grottoes on T'ai Shan. He hid in the nearby bushes transfixed by this stranger whose beauty was like a peony in full bloom. Each day, under the pretext of gathering wood, he left the other Immortals in the hermitage and crept down to the grotto to secretly gaze at her. After a week, he plucked up enough courage to talk to her. She was Pai Mou Tan, a young girl who had come to T'ai Shan in search of inner peace, but she too was distracted from her studies by Lu Tung Pin's charm and intelligence. Each time she sat down to contemplate the Taoist teachings her mind was distracted by thoughts of Lu Tung Pin and each time Lu Tung Pin sat down to discuss Taoism with the Eight Immortals he sat in a dream-like state, images of Pai Mou Tan flashing before his eyes.

Before long, Lu Tung Pin had broken the strict code of immortal behaviour; Pai Mou Tan was carrying his child. As a punishment, the Taoist qualifications he had earned through five hundred years of dedicated study were taken away from him. He had to prove his worth once again to the other Immortals.

Meanwhile Pai Mou Tan had become the laughing stock of the local people and was forced to abandon her studies. She moved far away to Tsou Lai Shan and set up home in a disbanded temple on the outskirts of the town. Not long after her arrival she gave birth to a boy who she named Pai Shih Lang.

Mother and child lived a quiet, secluded life, although they could not escape the jeers and taunts of the townspeople who had discovered their secret. By the age of nine Pai Shih Lang was a clever and quick-witted boy and each day he travelled alone to his school six miles away, crossing a wide stream on his outward and return journeys.

One morning, as he leaned down to take off his sandals before crossing the stream, he heard a man's voice quietly say, 'Don't take off your shoes, Pai Shih Lang. Climb on my back instead.'

Turning round, he saw an old bearded man sitting on the bank. He wore a black ragged cotton jacket and black cotton trousers rolled above the knee. His feet were resting in the stream's cool gurgling flow. Pai Shih Lang did as he was told. The same thing happened on his way home from school and continued to happen every day.

Several months later, in the twelfth month of the year, Pai Shih Lang's mother called her son into the kitchen and advised him.

'I have been thinking about your journey to and from school each day. Try not to get your feet too wet when you are crossing the stream, and, if they do get wet, dry them properly.'

'But I don't need to walk across the stream,' answered Pai Shih Lang mildly.

His surprised mother demanded an explanation and Pa Shih Lang dutifully recounted the whole story. After hearing what her son had to say, she told him to ask the old man the reason for his kindness.

The following day, as Pai Shih Lang was being carried across the stream he confronted the old man. 'You wait here for me every day, regardless of the weather. Why do you come and why do you carry me across the stream?'

The old man said nothing until he had reached the far side of the stream. He put Pai Shih Lang gently on the grass, looked him straight in the eyes and gave him this strange reply.

'I carry you because you have an important life ahead of you. One day you will be an emperor.'

Pai Mou Tan was delighted when her son told her about the old man's prediction, for she knew in her heart that her child was different from the thousands of other children in China.

Not long after, on the twenty-third day of the twelfth month, it was time to celebrate the kitchen god's ascent to heaven to visit the Jade Emperor. Pai Mou Tan spent all day cooking, cleaning and making ritual preparations, but it wasn't easy work without help from relatives or neighbours. Nobody ever visited them because they considered Pai Shih Lang an unnatural child. The townspeople would rather see them starve than lend them a bowl of rice. That evening Pai Mou Tan's problems increased when Pai Shih Lang came running home in tears.

'I am never going back to school again,' he cried as he fell into his mother's arms. 'All day long the boys mock me because I have no father.'

'Take no notice my son. Let them taunt you. They are only

jealous,' she said, gently stroking Pai Shih Lang's tear-stained face.

She gave him a bowl of dumplings to cheer him up. Her face was calm but her heart was furious. She had always worshipped the gods, yet her life was misery and unable to control herself anymore she grabbed a broom, ran into the kitchen and beat the statue of the kitchen god, crying tearfully.

'You wait and see, kitchen god. When my son becomes an emperor, I will take revenge. I will kill everyone who has ever mocked me and their blood will run like a river.'

In her temper she broke the kitchen god's nose and knocked out his front tooth and so the kitchen god rose to heaven in a battered and bloody state. As he bowed low before the Jade Emperor, the blood from his nose dripped on to the Emperor's golden shoes.

'What's happened to you,' asked the Emperor, slowly edging back from the kitchen god.

'Pai Shih Lang's mother beat me viciously. If her son becomes an emperor she will kill hundreds of people,' gasped the kitchen god, through swollen and battered lips.

'Oh, so that's her plan,' replied the Emperor. 'I know some humans are difficult but that's no reason for murdering them. She must be taught a lesson.'

The Jade Emperor spoke to the four generals who stood beside his throne. 'On the festival of the earth god's birthday, you must catch Pai Shih Lang and rip out the dragon sinews which give him immortal power. Every dragon sinew in his body must be torn away.'

Unaware of his fate, Pai Shih Lang continued to travel alone to school each day. But shortly before the earth god's birthday, the old man at the stream drew the small boy close to him.

'This is the last day I will carry you across the river. Your mother has been careless with the gods and your life is in trouble.'

The old man then told Pai Shih Lang everything about the kitchen god, the Jade Emperor and the punishment which lay in store for him.

'But you must save me! Please, I beg you to help me in any way you can,' cried Pai Shih Lang in terror.

'I can do nothing to prevent this punishment,' replied the old man. 'The Jade Emperor has given a command and it must be obeyed, but I can offer you some advice. When the guards start to rip out your dragon sinews, it will be excruciatingly painful because they are ripping out your immortality. But however painful it is, you must never scream or open your mouth. You must grit your teeth and endure this torture. They will take the strength from your body

The Kitchen God (from an early 19th-century Chinese woodcut)

but they will be unable to take your power of speech.'

As soon as the old man had finished speaking he disappeared into thin air, leaving Pai Shih Lang stunned and frightened. He realised the danger that lay in store and raced back home to tell his mother. She cuddled the little boy who was numb with terror, saying reassuringly, 'When the day arrives I will hide you in a safe place, so secret that not even the Jade Emperor can find you.'

And so they carefully counted the days to the earth god's festival, but unfortunately they counted a thirty day month instead of a twenty-nine day month. And so, mistakenly, Pai Shih Lang was sent to school on the second day of the second month, the day of his punishment.

As he crossed the fields, he noticed a black cloud moving slowly across the sky towards him. Suddenly a flash of lightning struck a tree three feet away from Pai Shih Lang and he realised with terror that his time had come. He spotted a nearby grave and ran for cover beneath the altar. He crept under the darkest corner of the altar and sat there shivering. But he could not fool the guards. The altar was smashed into fragments with a flash of lightning and the fiery-eyed guards descended from the heavens with a roll of thunder. They lifted Pai Shih Lang high into the air and with their bare hands they viciously ripped out his sinews one by one. Tears streamed down Pai Shih Lang's face but he did not utter a single sound. When every dragon sinew had been torn away they threw Pai Shih Lang to the ground and disappeared into the heavens as quickly as they had come.

For a long time Pai Shih Lang lay on the ground, unable to move. Finally he gathered enough strength to pull himself to his feet and staggered home. But the Jade Emperor had not completely destroyed his power, he still had immortal power in his dragon teeth and jade mouth.

Pai Shih Lang Ensnares the Gods

After being punished, Pai Shih Lang never left his home. He grew to hate the gods with a deep vengence, for if the kitchen god had not gossiped to the Jade Emperor he would still have complete power. Pai Shih Lang's only worldly possession was a gourd, a present from his mother, so he decided to use this to exact revenge. He went into the kitchen and bellowed to the kitchen god, 'Get into this bottle, you slanderer and liar!'

The kitchen god was helpless against the power of Pai Shih Lang's dragon voice and with a gust of wind he entered the gourd. Everything that Pai Shih Lang said was recognised as the truth by the gods and they had to obey.

From that day onwards, Pai Shih Lang travelled the world ensnaring every god who crossed his path. He discovered gods on rocky mountain sides, in wooded valleys, deep in rivers and on wide open plains. No god on the earth could refuse his command. After years of wandering, he arrived at T'ai Shan town in Shantung province. The town lay at the foot of the mountain where he had been conceived.

The wily goddess, Pi Hsia Yan Chun, was staying in the oldest temple in the town and had calculated the arrival of Pai Shih Lang. She sent four strong fire dragons to surround Pai Shih Lang before he entered the town. The dragons flew across the town and landed in a field where Pai Shih Lang was resting. They formed a circle of unbearable white heat around the field, completely immobilising Pai Shih Lang. But Pai Shih Lang was too hungry and exhausted to put up a fight and the only thought on his mind was food. In the corner of the field a woman was sowing seeds in the freshly tilled soil. At her feet lay a basket covered with a cotton cloth.

'Old woman, can you help me?' he cried. 'I have not eaten for three days. I will do anything for you if you give me a morsel of food.'

The old woman looked up from her work and slowly approached the hungry stranger. 'I would help you if I could,' she said, 'but I only have one pancake and a bowl of rice soup for my son who has been working in the fields since dawn.'

Pai Shih Lang persisted with his request. 'If you do not feed me, I will die. Just look at me. I am so thin the skin is hanging from my bones. You cannot leave me to die.'

The old woman shrugged her shoulders and replied, 'Why should I feed an absolute stranger. You are not my cousin, you are not my friend, you are not my son. What right have you to make these demands?'

She paused for a moment and then continued, 'If you kneel down and bow before me three times, calling me mother each time, I will give you food and water.'

In desperation Pai Shih Lang obeyed her and in return the satisfied woman gave him the pancake and bowl of rice. Pai Shih Lang fell upon the food devouring it with an unquenchable appetite. Only when he had finished eating the food did he look up to discover that the old woman and the fire dragons had disappeared.

Pai Shih Lang continued on his travels without a second thought to the events of the day. He worked his way through the temples in T'ai Shan town, snapping up gods and immortals at every opportunity and then he started his ascent of T'ai Shan mountain. The gods quivered in the grottoes and the immortals shook in the caves but there was no escape, with just one word from Pai Shih Lang they were trapped forever in the gourd. After a successful afternoon's hunting Pai Shih Lang reached the summit of T'ai Shan where he was greeted by the sight of a breathtaking gold and jade palace. Above the doorway hung a sign 'Pi Hsia Temple'. He fearlessly entered the temple courtyard where the goddess Pi Hsia Yan Chun sat in glory on a lotus flower throne.

He reached for the gourd hanging from his waist but before he touched it she demanded, 'What do you think you are doing, Pai Shih Lang? Have you gone mad? Do you not recognise me as the old woman who fed and watered you less than four hours ago in the field. You called me mother three times and although you can imprison the other gods you cannot ensnare your mother.'

Pai Shih Lang was left speechless. How could he even think of threatening the woman he had called mother. In shame he knelt before her to apologise but as he knelt on the marble floor his gourd hit the ground and smashed into a hundred pieces.

Out came thousands of gods, tumbling on top of one another in a frenzy. Dazed and excited they dashed about the palace ecstatically. They climbed out of the windows, rushed through the doors, jumped into rivers, ran into caves and hid in grottoes. The mountain was alive with gods dashing backwards and forwards.

Pai Shih Lang lay in despair on the marble floor but the gods didn't look back. The most important thing for them was to hide before he pulled himself together and thought of a new trick. Hundreds of gods and immortals had headed towards the nearest cottage and the nearest grotto. They pushed and pulled each other as they tried to jam into every available space. Pi Hsia Yan Chun watched them with satisfaction, but when she tried to count the number of gods who had squeezed into these two places she became totally confused. Instead she made an estimate, she named the cottage 'The Ten Thousand Immortals Cottage' and she named the grotto 'The Thousand Buddha Grotto'. To this day people come to visit the gods and immortals here. Only the kitchen god ran back to find a warm, safe hiding place on the kitchen stove. He was in a good position there to watch everything that went on in the house. Even now people are afraid that he might gossip to the Jade Emperor if they are unkind, angry or deceitful. To prevent him spreading rumours they pin two poems to the kitchen wall. One says 'When you go up to heaven, speak only good words' and the other says 'When you come down from heaven, bring only good fortune'.

Pai Shih Lang is Forgiven

When Pai Shih Lang had finally recovered from the shock of the broken gourd and the rampaging gods, Pi Hsia Yan Chun summoned him to her side.

'My boy, you have brought thousands of gods and immortals to me and it is the Jade Emperor's wish that I govern them kindly. The time is now right for you to see your father, Lu Tung Pin, again. He is ready to forgive you and welcome you into his arms. You will find him meditating in a cave at the foot of this mountain.' Pai Shih Lang rushed off eagerly to see the father he had never known. He approached a deep river at the foot of the mountain and at its shallowest point he heard a rustling noise in the reeds on the opposite side. Looking up he saw his father standing there with outstretched arms. Before Pai Shih Lang could open his mouth, his father spoke.

'My son, I am waiting here for you. Do not be afraid. If you take my hand you will be safe.'

Pai Shih Lang stretched out his hand towards his father and the moment that their fingers touched Pai Shih Lang disappeared. Pai Shih Lang had returned to his father's body. But Pai Shih Lang was not forgotten. To this day, the village where he lived is called Pai Temple village and the place he called home is now famous as Pai Shih Lang Temple.

The Dream of Lu Tung Pin

The Immortal, Han Chung Li was one day travelling from the old imperial capital city of Ch'ang-an, when he stopped off at an inn along the road. It was an inn reserved mostly for the use of officials travelling the busy road to the capital. Han Chung Li settled down with a jug of warmed wine and watched the officials come and go.

It so happened that Lu Tung Pin was travelling along the same road that very day. He had not yet become an immortal and was still an official in the government, destined for great honour and power. His family had been high ranking officials for generations, so it was natural that he should become one. Even when he was at the first stage of the civil examinations, he showed himself to be a most skilful writer and thinker. Men marked him out for high office and he was content to go that way. Yet he also had a deep interest in the ways of the wise men and of the immortals. Whenever he could, he would study the ancient writings and meditate on his life and its purpose. But official duties left him little time for such reflections and he was still too dazzled by the hoped-for glories of power to seriously contemplate giving everything up and becoming a hermit.

So it was, that on that day Lu Tung Pin came into the inn, his mind full of the possibilities of promotion. Han Chung Li saw the young man enter and seeing that he was made of different mettle from the rest of the officials, invited him to sit and drink with him. Lu Tung Pin accepted gladly and ordered a clean cup for the warmed wine. The two men sat and chatted about the ways of the world and soon moved on to discuss the path of immortality and the Way. Han Chung Li could see that here was a man who was very close to becoming an immortal, but who was still dazzled by power.

Han Chung Li drew the little heater to him and began to warm the wine. Lu Tung Pin found that the fumes of the warming wine and the effects of the journey made him very sleepy. Before he knew what was happening he was fast asleep.

As he slept, he had a most convincing dream. He saw himself returning from his journey and being promoted to a very senior office. From there he rose within a few years to the most senior post in the Emperor's court. For fifty years he was favoured and blessed by fortune. Emperors listened to his word, governments quaked at his anger and favours were bestowed at his command. But it was not to last. One day he offended the new Emperor, who, tired of this powerful man, was delighted to have an excuse to dismiss him. Immediately his enemies closed in. The Emperor was told alarming tales of Lu Tung Pin's plans and ambitions. Soon the Emperor was convinced that Lu Tung Pn was an enemy of the state. Summoning Lu Tung Pin, he ordered him into exile. But worse was to come. Shortly afterwards, the Emperor ordered that the whole of Lu Tung Pin's family be executed. Not a single one was spared.

Alone, exiled and mourning for his murdered family, Lu Tung Pin sat sighing bitterly in a faraway country, when suddenly he woke up. He was still in the inn and the wine was not even hot yet!

The shock of the dream was enough to convince Lu Tung Pin that the way of power was not the true Way. Realising how temporary and fickle are the ways of men, he decided to follow Han Chung Li and to study the ways of the immortals. So he left his servants and the task he had been sent to do and went with Han Chung Li up into the Ho Ling mountains. Here he cast aside forever the stern expression of the high official. Year by year he studied with Han Chung Li, until he had learnt the divine mysteries. At the end of many years of practice, he did indeed become an immortal.

The Oil Seller

Lu Tung Pin liked to travel about in disguise to test the honesty of people on earth. It was always his joy to give to those who were honest the understanding of the Tao and the chance of immortality.

One day he decided to become an oil seller. Dressing himself up and carrying his barrels of oil, he set off to find anyone who would accept his measure of oil for a fixed and just price.

At first he was very hopeful and journeyed to the nearby city to sell his wares. The first house he went up to was a very grand place so he knocked at the main door. The doorman opened it and scowled at Lu Tung Pin.

'What do you want?' he demanded.

'To sell you a little oil,' replied Lu Tung Pin.

'Then get round to the back door. Only gentlemen come through this door.' And so saying he suddenly lashed out with his boot and kicked Lu Tung Pin down the stairs.

Picking himself up, Lu Tung Pin trudged round to the back door. But he got little encouragement there. The doorman had already told the kitchen staff about the oil seller who had come to the front door. When Lu Tung Pin knocked, he was treated as a joke and the rubbish was tipped over him. Filled with anger, Lu Tung Pin was tempted to strike the whole house down. But he decided to leave them to their own foolish ways.

Over the next few days, he tried to sell his oil in the market place. Everyone wanted to barter with him but when he told them that the price was fixed, no-one would believe him. They were sure that he must be trying to trick them, so they would not buy.

Lu Tung Pin soon tired of the city and thought that he might be better off in a smaller place. So he travelled to the nearby town and approached the smartest house. Remembering his painful experience in the city, he knocked at the back door. A friendly young woman opened the door and asked what he was selling. He told her he was selling oil. Suddenly a gruff voice sounded from within the house. 'Who is at the door?' The young woman looked frightened and said it was an oil seller. 'Tell him to come in,' said the gruff voice.

The Oil Seller

When Lu Tung Pin came inside the biggest man he had ever seen was seated at a table. 'How much are you charging for your oil?' asked the man. When he heard what Lu Tung Pin was charging, he frowned and said, 'I'll give you half your price.' When Lu Tung Pin refused, he said, 'Then I will take it anyway,' and he rose to his feet with a menacing look on his face.

Lu Tung Pin was not sure what to do. He could see the woman was very frightened, so he decided to face up to this bully. Lu Tung Pin whisked his fly whisk out and waved it in the giant's direction. There was a loud bang and the giant disappeared. Bowing politely to the terrified woman, he made his way out of the house and decided that perhaps the town was not the right place for him either. So he went to the local village.

But he fared no better in the village. People tried to trick him or simply ignored him. Eventually, after weeks of wandering and trying, he came at last to an isolated country lane. As he passed a tiny, tumbledown farm, a woman ran out to him. 'Please can I buy some oil from you, for I have almost none left?' Lu Tung Pin hesitated. He did not want to say yes, because he was afraid that the woman would not have enough money to pay the fair price. But he had to stick to what he had agreed with himself. So he named his price. To his astonishment and delight, the woman agreed and ran back to get the money.

Lu Tung Pin followed her and saw the poverty of her house and little farm. As the woman was finding the coins, Lu Tung Pin took a few grains of rice and threw them into the well. Then he turned and received the money and gave the woman her oil. With that he wished her well and went on his way. It was not until later that day that the woman went to draw water from the well. Imagine her astonishment when she found the well did not give her water, but wine! She drew another bucket full. More wine! She soon discovered that whenever she drew water, it was wine.

Within weeks she opened a wine shop. People came from miles around to buy her wine, for it had a most wonderful taste. Within a very short time, she was able to rebuild her farm and within a year or two, she was one of the wealthiest people in the area and much sought after by the eligible bachelors of the area. And all this came about because she had been honest.

Shaoshing's Aromatic Pastries

Heng the baker was known by everyone in Hangchow as Hsaio Shaoshing, the little one of Shaoshing. His ancestors were buried in Shaoshing district but he had always lived in the nearby town of Hangchow. After his father's death, Hsaio Shaoshing carried on the family tradition as Hangchow's aromatic pastry maker. He made steamed rice pastries in the family's small straw roofed cottage at the foot of Mount Cheng. Although his cakes were popular he made a meagre living, just enough to support himself and his blind mother.

Before dawn he rose to grind rice for his steamed pastries. Each day he sold his pastries from door-to-door down Hangchow's narrow streets. Each afternoon he returned home carrying a few unsold cakes. Hsaio Shaoshing was an obedient son. He never ate these unsold cakes but gave them to his mother.

Each New Year, the people of the town wished each other health, happiness and prosperity. It was Hsaio Shaoshing's busiest time of the year. The pronunciation of the Chinese word for cake was the same as the pronunciation for the word promotion and so the villagers believed that the cakes would confer good fortune for the coming year.

One New Year, the villagers formed long queues to buy the pastries but Heng obediently put one aside for his mother. When evening fell, Heng returned home. His empty straw baskets were thrown across his shoulder, but in the pocket of his cotton jacket was one pastry. Suddenly an old man in ragged clothes stepped out from the shadows and blocked his path.

'Have you anything to eat?' begged the old man.

Heng could not turn the old man away empty-handed so he offered him a brass coin.

The old man shook his head and said quietly, 'I do not need money. I need food. Give me the cake in your basket.'

Heng was confused. The beggar looked tired and hungry, but his mother was also tired and hungry. He did not want to see anyone suffer, but who was the most needy? His mother would forgive him. He would bake her an extra cake tomorrow, but the beggar might starve. Heng gave him the cake. The beggar nodded his head in thanks and disappeared into the shadows.

As dusk fell the following evening, the beggar appeared again with the same request. Heng did not refuse him. The beggar continued to appear on the following forty-nine days and each time Heng, without hesitation, gave him a cold pastry. On the fiftieth day the beggar sensed an unhappiness in Heng's voice and enquired, 'What is troubling you my friend? You are walking in a dark cloud.'

'Thank you for your concern, but you are more helpless than I,' replied Heng. 'Each day the mists hang low over the village. The rain runs in torrents from the roofs and in the streets. Who will buy my cakes in this weather? The women barely open their doors to let their children in, so why should they give time to me. Each evening I return with a basket of cold cakes which my mother eats and now she is sick and it is my fault.

The beggar laughed at Heng's misery. 'Look at me,' he said. 'I have eaten your cakes every day. Am I ill?' While speaking he pulled open the drawstring on a worn pigskin bag and drew out a small green bottle of tablets. He handed the bottle to Heng.

'Give one of these tablets to your mother and put another in your mixing bowl each morning. Do not ask any questions. You have been kind to me, now let me help you.' Then, a wind rose up lashing the rain against Heng's face and he lifted his arm to shield his eyes. The wind disappeared as quickly as it had arisen and when Heng opened his eyes the beggar had gone.

Heng did as he had been told. He ground a tablet with rice powder and placed a bowl of cakes in a large steaming pan. Within a few minutes a delicious aroma filled the air.

His mother called from her chair, 'What is that fragrant aroma? Why do your cakes smell so sweet?'

'I have put a strange tablet in my cakes. You must eat one, mother', replied Heng.

She ate one as he had requested and within minutes her sickness had disappeared. Heng cried out in joy.

'I knew it. I am sure of it. That was no ordinary beggar. That was an Immortal!'

Heng revealed all that had happened but the one thing he could not reveal was the beggar's name.

'Tell me,' said his mother, 'did he beg any differently to other beggars?'

Heng tried to remember everything about the old man. He had seen him sleeping in the dark temple doorway using two rice bowls as a pillow but he could think of nothing unusual about the beggar.

'But that is it,' cried his mother. 'When two mouths join together they form the character Lu, likewise when two bowls join together they form the character Lu. You have been talking to Lu Tung Pin, one of the Eight Immortals.

From that day on the villagers were eager to try the 'immortal pastries'. They were the sweetest pastries in the province and people gathered round Heng's door to learn the art of making such fine aromatic pastries. His fame spread quickly and before long his pastries were known as Shaoshing pastries. The 'little man from Shaoshing' no longer trudged the streets selling his pastries. He had earned enough money to open a shop and above the door hung the sign 'Hsaio Shaoshing's Aromatic Pastry Shop' and to this day Shaoshing is famous for its aromatic pastries.

Lu Tung Pin's Vengence

Although the Eight Immortals dedicated their lives to the needy and the poor, they were by no means perfect. They all had their weaknesses and faults, especially Lu Tung Pin, the youngest and the least experienced. He could be boastful, proud and a bad loser.

One summer Lu Tung Pin was travelling by boat down the Ou river, playing chess with the helmsman to relieve his boredom. After a competitive game the helmsman finally won. Lu Tung Pin was so angry and humiliated that he shot the chess set into the water. From that time on, there was a mountain on the banks of the Ou river that was shaped like a chess set.

The following summer, Lu Tung Pin returned to the Ou river determined to exact revenge upon the helmsman and any inhabitants of the Ou river. He filled two huge baskets with soil, tied the baskets to an iron pole, laid the pole across his shoulders and set off with the intention of blocking the flow of the Ou river. Just as he reached the fields bordering the river, he was stopped by an old farmer.

'Stranger, I need your help,' cried the old farmer. 'My pig has just escaped and I am too old to run after it. Could you catch it for me?'

Lu Tung Pin carefully laid his baskets and pole on the floor and ran after the pig. When he had disappeared behind the farmhouse, the farmer swopped the iron pole for a wooden pole. Not long after Lu Tung Pin returned with the squealing pig in his arms. He tied the pig to a gate post, said his goodbyes and heaved the pole and baskets on to his shoulder. There was a resounding crack as the pole split into two pieces and the baskets of soil rolled across the floor. The soil flew out in all directions and when the baskets finally came to a standstill, there was a large mound of soil, big enough to hide the farmer's field of sweet potatoes from view.

Lu Tung Pin couldn't believe his misfortune and was more determined than ever to wreak havoc on the villagers of this district. He travelled to the widest part of the Ou river and there he decided on the perfect revenge. He took a magic duster from his pigskin bag and shook it at a pile of earthenware jars lying on a nearby hillside. There was a streak of lightning and the jars immediately changed into a flock of white sheep. Lu Tung Pin then changed his duster into a stout walking stick and drove the sheep to a small hamlet of low wooden houses clustered around a shallow part of the river. He carefully made his way across the slippery stepping stones to the far side of the river. The sheep slipped and staggered after him, but it took so long for them to cross that Lu Tung Pin settled himself on a nearby rock and patiently waited for them.

While he sat there a woodcutter and his friend approached the far side of the river and stood close to the river bank waiting for the sheep to cross. The sheep seemed to be taking forever and, since the night was quickly closing in, the woodcutter asked Lu Tung Pin to part his sheep so that he could cross the stream before darkness fell. Lu Tung Pin waded to the far side of the river to prevent the remaining sheep from crossing the river and, as he did so, he recognised the helmsman he had met on his previous visits to the Ou river, standing behind the woodcutter. The woodcutter nodded his head gratefully to Lu Tung Pin and started to cross the river, but, before he could reach the opposite side, his way was blocked by a lame sheep. As he stood waiting for the sheep to cross, the bundle of wood on his back became heavier and heavier and the bones in his back felt as though they were being crushed by two heavy stones. The woodcutter turned to Lu Tung Pin for help but the moment he saw the mischievous smile on the wily immortal's face, he knew that he had been tricked. The woodcutter became nervous and hit the sheep in front of him with his walking stick. The lame sheep slipped off the mossy stepping stone into the water, but the moment it touched the water it changed into an earthenware jar. Lu Tung Pin was furious, he jumped up and scrambled across the stones to the old man.

'You fool, you idiot!' he cried. You'll have to pay a high price for killing one of my sheep.'

But the woodcutter was not so easily defeated. 'It is only an earthenware jar,' he protested. 'Why are you calling it a sheep? What kind of evil are you up to? I've a good mind to report you to the judge.'

Lu Tung Pin was anxious to avoid trouble with a human judge and all the local people so he quickly changed his tone of voice.

'Hold on. Let's not be hasty. Why don't we negotiate? I will tell you a secret that you must not repeat to any other living being. I am Lu Tung Pin, one of the Eight Immortals and these earthenware jars are sheep. We are on our way to block the river so that the lowlands on either side will be flooded. I'm giving you a chance to escape.

You should take this opportunity now!'

The woodcutter's first thought was for the safety of the citizens, but he hid his intention from Lu Tung Pin. The woodcutter calmly crossed the remaining stones and as soon as he reached the other side he let out an almighty yell.

'Come quickly, everybody. Leave your houses. Lu Tung Pin is trying to murder you. Save yourselves now. Come as fast as you can!'

The villagers came rushing from their houses, brandishing wooden brushes and hoes, and raced towards the stream. Some sheep ran wildly across the hillside, some fell into the water and others just huddled close to the bank, but none could escape the villagers' determined blows. As each sheep was struck, it fell to the floor and turned into a broken earthenware pottery jar. While the villagers beat the sheep, the woodcutter lunged ferociously at Lu Tung Pin and caught him on the leg with his wooden staff. Lu Tung Pin hobbled away as fast as his wounded leg could carry him, but each time he tried to fly to heaven he fell to the ground. Finally, after concentrating all his energy in his legs, he managed to leap successfully into the air and escaped to heaven. Lu Tung Pin had learnt his lesson and didn't dare try to block the Ou river again. Meanwhile the villagers threw all the jars into a nearby lake and the wine that remained at the bottom of the jars seeped into the water. To this day, the water in the lake smells like wine and it is popularly known as 'Wine Lake'.

A Matchmaker for Kuan Yin

Kuan Yin, the goddess of mercy, decided to build a bridge for the townspeople of Ch'uan Chou near the eastern capital, Lo-yang. The building was subsidised by donations she collected when wandering the country in different disguises. She sometimes stood as a beautiful young woman in the brow of a boat, encouraging passersby on the banks of the river to throw coins. She vowed to marry the man whose coins landed on her body.

One day Lu Tung Pin happened to be in the same town as Kuan Yin. In the disguise of a wrinkled white haired old man he pushed his way into the bustling crowd watching Kuan Yin's boat glide by.

A group of handsome wealthy men stood at the front of the crowd throwing handfuls of bronze and silver coins at Kuan Yin. Each took careful aim but always missed Kuan Yin. Some coins hit the helmsman, some landed in the bottom of the boat and some fell in the river where little children were waiting to dive in and recover them.

Lu Tung Pin immediately recognised the goddess of mercy. 'She is playing a dangerous game,' he thought. 'She will never marry a human but the young men will have to discover that for themselves.'

There was one impoverished young man in the crowd who was destined to discover the truth. Wei T'o, a straw shoe vendor, had become totally enamoured of Kuan Yin after one glimpse of her flowing black hair and cherry blossom lips. Lu Tung Pin followed Wei T'o's gaze and understood his desire. He whispered encouragingly over the young man's shoulder, 'Why don't you try to win her hand in marriage?' Wei T'o swung round to face Lu Tung Pin, his face covered with confusion and embarassment.

'Please do not mock me. I have worked night and day to make extra money to give as a donation. Last time I gave a donation towards a bridge the government misused the funding. This time I know Kuan Yin will use the money wisely, but I would never be able to throw this silver coin into her hands.'

Lu Tung Pin listened carefully to Wei T'o's words and knew him to be an honourable man. At the risk of incurring Kuan Yin's anger, he decided to help him.

'Pick up that large stone,' he commanded, pointing at a stone

Kuan Yin, Goddess of Mercy (from a late 19th-century Chinese woodcut)

lying near his feet. 'Now throw it at your silver coin.'

Wei T'o threw the stone with all his strength and smashed the coin into tiny fragments. As he stooped down to pick up the powder-like fragments he heard the helmsman shout, 'The sky is turning dark, three days are nearly over and the lady must return to her home before nightfall. This is your last chance to win her heart and her hand.'

'Hurry up! Throw your coins now,' cried Lu Tung Pin to Wei T'o.

Wei T'o stood on the edge of the bank, closed his eyes for a moment in prayer and then threw the coins at Kuan Yin. Miraculously they landed on her hair, shoulders, feet and in her hands. A huge cheer rose from the crowd who lifted Wei T'o into the air in congratulations. Kuan Yin stood in the prow of the boat, stunned and speechless. Gazing into the crowd she caught sight of Lu Tung Pin's mischievous smile and was on the verge of disappearing into thin air until she remembered her promise. 'The citizens have entrusted their money to me and I am duty bound to build the bridge.' And so she ordered the helmsman to row the boat closer to the riverbank and held out her hand to Wei T'o. As the boat drew nearer Wei T'o reluctantly jumped aboard and Lu Tung Pin followed. Wei T'o shifted uneasily from foot to foot, eyes lowered to avoid Kuan Yin's soul searching gaze. Lu Tung Pin brusquely interrupted the scene.

'The great goddess wanted to marry a young man. Well here he is! You have me to thank as your matchmaker.'

Lu Tung Pin's words made Kuan Yin angry and embarrassed. He had put her in a hopeless situation, but she was a goddess and must keep her word. While she quietly considered the best course of action the helmsman gave a cry of recognition.

'Why it's Wei T'o. Do you not remember him, my goddess? He worked his fingers to the bone to provide money for a bridge but the government misused the funding.'

Kuan Yin softened at the helmsman's words, but nevertheless she had been tricked by Lu Tung Pin and had to find an escape route.

She called Wei T'o and the helmsman to her side and spoke reassuringly to them. 'I respect both of you and entrust the bridge-building into your capable hands. Once Lo-yang bridge has been constructed I will marry as promised.'

Meanwhile Lu Tung Pin lost interest in the proceedings and slowly rose upwards from the boat in a mass of grey smoke. The others watched as he gradually disappeared into the heavens. Wei T'o now had the courage and determination to build the bridge singlehandedly. He set up a makeshift home nearer the site Kuan Yin had chosen and with the helmsman worked from dawn to dusk each day of the year. Even when the other workers returned home, Wei T'o and the helmsman worked by the light of a small oil lamp. After two years, a beautiful arched stone bridge had been constructed and everyone in the province was invited to the opening party.

Kuan Yin did not forget her promise. She was there to celebrate the opening and to thank the two men for the dedication they had shown. After a day of feasting, singing and dancing, the tired villagers drifted back home leaving Kuan Yin and Wei T'o alone on the bridge.

'Take my hand,' said Kuan Yin gently. 'Do not be afraid. You have proved your worth and I am ready to take you as my husband.' Before Wei T'o could utter a word he felt his feet rise from the ground. This happened slowly at first but then he rose faster and faster away from the earth. Kuan Yin kept tightly hold of his hand and when he did pluck up the courage to look down, the villages, mountains and rivers looked like small toys. They flew on and on until they arrived at Kuan Yin's home, Pu T'o Shan. She brought him down to earth gently in a green meadow.

'Sit opposite me,' said Kuan Yin softly.

Wei T'o sat crosslegged opposite the beautiful goddess. She continued to speak reassuringly. 'You know that we cannot have a normal human marriage but do not worry. You and I will sit like this, facing each other for eternity. Mountains may crumble and cities disappear but you have won my heart for all time and I will never leave you.'

To this day, in temples throughout China, prayers are said before statues of Kuan Yin and Wei T'o facing each other and whenever two people meet and declare undying love, the Chinese say they are 'face-to-face husband and wife'.

The Path to Immortality

Ti Kuai Li and the Woodcutter's Daughter

Ti Kuai Li lived in a mountain cave and worked a small plot of land around his home. One day while he was planting seeds, a woodcutter approached his cave. Ti Kuai Li offered him food and a humble meal and together they sat in the shade of a tree. The woodcutter told Ti Kuai Li many strange things.

'You will have a long life and you will be a learned man. You will bring happiness and comfort to many people. One day you will become one of the Eight Immortals and will be taken away from this bitter sea of human troubles.'

Ti Kuai Li sat silently for a while and then said, 'This is a difficult task, a task that will take many years. I don't expect a long life and I've never searched for immortality. However I do want to learn the reason for life and this is why I'll study hard.'

The woodcutter was pleased with Ti Kuai Li's words but said nothing. Finally as the sun began to set the woodcutter spoke.

'I don't understand Taoism myself, but I have an obedient daughter who wants me to live a long and healthy life and in order to bless me with long life she wishes to become a nun. Will you let her be your student, so that she can serve you in your cave?'

Ti Kuai Li lifted his head quickly. 'No, I cannot do that,' he said.

'But why not?' asked the woodcutter.

Ti Kuai Li shook his head again. 'I am still learning. How can I have a student when I myself am only a student?'

The woodcutter nodded thoughtfully. 'You may be right,' he agreed.

Several days later, as the first stars began to appear in the sky, the woodcutter came to see Ti Kuai Li again. Although the shadows of evening had come down, Ti Kuai Li could make out a beautfiul girl standing next to the woodcutter.

'This is my daughter. I have told her that you are still studying, but she wants to be your student and begged me to bring her to you. I told her not to come, but she refused to eat unless she could study with you. What can I do with such a determined girl. You're my only hope, so please promise that you will be her master.'

Ti Kuai Li closed his eyes and ignored her. The woodcutter turned to his daughter saying, 'Stay here and obey him. I'm leaving. Don't try to follow me.'

And with this order the woodcutter turned quickly and soon disappeared into the shadow of the trees. For a long time there was a silence between the woodcutter's daughter and Ti Kuai Li. She did not raise her head to look at him, but she slowly walked towards him and knelt at his feet.

Still Ti Kuai Li did not pay any attention. She felt uncertain and looked around for something to do. Ti Kuai Li sat silently reading his Taoist books while she picked up a brush and swept the floor. In the candlelight of the cave she could see Ti Kuai Li's handsome face and every now and then she stopped to stare at him, but all this time he did not even glance at her. Cautiously and respectfully she approached him.

'Master, I know that you are studying hard, but do you not think that you should also have a family? Do you have one?'

Ti Kuai Li remained silent. The woodcutter's daughter tried to make him speak once again.

'Are you married? Do you have any problems? Please tell me what is wrong with you. You know that I'm here to help you, not to harm you. Talk to me. Your most precious thoughts will be safe with me.'

But Ti Kuai Li's eyes were lowered as he stood up and walked away. The girl continued unabashed.

'Please listen to me. I don't want to learn Taoism but my father is forcing me to marry an ugly man. He has long dark eyebrows, huge ears and in one ear he wears a heavy brass ring. He is not only ugly but his body is twisted and mishapen. How could I ever marry him? I would rather learn Taoism than lead a miserable life with this man, so I will keep my promise to my father and study with you. But if I could marry a handsome man like you, I would obey my father and have a good husband at the same time.'

Still Ti Kuai Li said nothing. He sat quietly looking at his books.

'But Master Li, are you shy? Why don't you abandon your studies. How can you live in a cold cave? It's a lonely and difficult life. Look at me. Don't you find me attractive. Why not come to the town with me and enjoy the pleasures it has to offer?'

Still Ti Kuai Li did not move. He did not look at her and he did not make a sound. By this time the girl had become exhausted. She had tried to make him speak, she had tried to draw him away from his studies but had failed and, in desperation, she sat in a dark corner of the cave. That night, storm clouds hung low in the sky and she shivered from the sharp wind blowing through the cave entrance. She stood up, pulled her thin cotton jacket over her shoulders and once more tried to please Ti Kuai Li. She huddled close to him, urging him to choose a wife. But no amount of persuasion or gentle words could move Ti Kuai Li. Early next morning the woodcutter returned as Ti Kuai Li was working in his garden.

'Where is my daughter?' he shouted.

Ti Kuai Li put down his shovel and looked at the woodcutter. 'I don't know. The girl disappeared in the night.'

'Did you try to rape her? Then did you try to kill her? Tell me, tell me. You cannot lie to me,' shouted the woodcutter angrily.

But Ti Kuai Li replied calmly, 'I would never do such a wicked thing.'

A smile came to the woodcutter's face and he took hold of Ti Kuai Li's hand. 'I believe you. You have a good understanding of Taoism. You and I are alike.'

And before Ti Kuai Li stood a man in a dark red robe and he knew at once it was Lao Tzu. In his hand he held a piece of wood. 'I made the girl from this wood. I tried to trap you Ti Kuai Li, but you are too determined and strong to be fooled by trickery.'

Lao Tzu put his hand in the leather satchel he carried at his side and took out a small white tablet which he handed to Ti Kuai Li.

'Eat it and do not ask any questions.'

Lao Tzu then turned his back and walked down the hill away from the cave. Ti Kuai Li swallowed the pill and from that time onwards he was never hungry or ill. For many years he travelled the country helping the sick and the poor. He travelled day and night occasionally returning home to his cave where he studied and meditated upon the Taoist teachings.

Ti Kuai Li is Given the Gift of Flight

One day, as Ti Kuai Li sat at the entrance of his cave, he noticed two men stealthily entering a hut that was built on the edge of his fields. He watched as they forced open the floor boards with an axe and hid two heavy bags on the earth below. Every now and then they looked up nervously to see if they were being watched. Once the boards had been replaced, they ran down the hill glancing back occasionally at the hut. Ti Kuai Li saw everything but did nothing. Later that day Ti Kuai Li visited a teashop in the town at the foot of the hill. As he sat sipping green tea he was approached by a white bearded man.

Lao Tzu (from a late 19th-century Chinese woodcut)

'Do you mind if I join you?' asked the old man.

Without waiting for a reply, he sat opposite Ti Kuai Li and looked at him carefully. After several minutes he spoke. 'I can tell from your face that one day you will be very rich.'

Ti Kuai Li thought to himself, 'Yes, I could well become rich, since I know where stolen money is hidden.'

The old man urged him to take any money that came his way, regardless of its source, for without money he would be bitter and unhappy.

'Who are you?' asked Ti Kuai Li.

'My name is Ywen Yau,' replied the old man. But he did not offer any more information.

Eventually Ti Kuai Li spoke up. 'Yes, I know where two stolen money bags are hidden, but why should I steal that money myself. I do not care if I am poor for ever.'

'But don't you want a prosperous life?' insisted the old man.

Ti Kuai Li shrugged his shoulders. Why did he need wealth? What would he do with money? He was happy as he was and he did not care. Several days later Ti Kuai Li met the old man again in the darkened doorway of a temple. This time Ywen Yau gave him a tablet taken from a small cowskin purse hanging from his waist. 'Swallow this,' he said.

Ti Kuai Li did as he was told. As soon as he had swallowed the pill, he felt a strange feeling inside. He began to walk down the road and suddenly, instead of walking at his normal speed, he seemed to be travelling faster than a swallow. He began to run and then, before he knew it, his feet were raised from the ground
and he could feel his body flying across the sky, high above the houses. The old man had not been a fortune teller. He was Lao Tzu. Once again he had come to teach him and to help him.

Ti Kuai Li is Given the Gift of Immortality

Ti Kuai Li had been given a priceless gift by Lao Tzu. He could now fly faster than the swiftest bird and walk more than a thousand miles a day. He used this gift wisely, dedicating his life to the sick and the poor. Years spent studying the Taoist teachings had made Ti Kuai Li a learned man and at Lao Tzu's request he accepted a student, Li Ching, a young boy from a nearby province.

One morning, as they were studying together in the cave, he told his student, 'Today I will go to Wah Shan mountain. I have an appointment with Lao Tzu. Do not worry. I'll return tomorrow.'

The student was shocked. 'But how can you return tomorrow? Wah Shan is five thousand miles from here. How can you travel that distance so quickly? It would take me many months to walk there.'

'Don't ask any more questions,' said Ti Kuai Li. 'My soul is going to travel there, but I will leave my body at home with you. My soul can travel much quicker. If I do not return in seven days, do not worry because I will have become immortal and you can then burn my body because I will no longer need it.'

Ti Kuai Li sat still in meditation. As the student watched him, curls of smoke appeared above Ti Kuai Li's head. The student approached his master and held a finger beneath his nose, but could not feel his breath. His master had left him. For six and a half days Li Ching cared for Ti Kuai Li's body, but on the afternoon of the seventh day Li Ching received a letter from his mother begging him to come as quickly as possible. She was mortally ill and wanted to see her son for the last time. What could Li Ching do? He needed to see his mother and six and a half days had passed without news of his master. Li Ching remembered his master's words – 'If I do not return in seven days, you can then burn my body' – and in haste to see his dying mother he burnt his master's body.

No sooner had he left the cave, when he saw a beggar dying on the roadside. He knelt at his side, but there was little he could do as the beggar's breathing was slow and coarse. The dying man had large ears and in one he wore a thick brass earring. His hair was short and his eyebrows were long, scraggy and dark. On his head he wore a pan lid and his leg was disfigured and bleeding. As Li Ching knelt there, the beggar died. But he had no time to bury him. He had to rush to his mother.

'If I'm late my mother will die and I will never see her. I must go quickly and then return to bury the beggar.'

No sooner was he out of sight of the cave, when Ti Kuai Li arrived to reclaim his body. But where was his body? His soul hovered for several minutes above the straw mattress where he had last seen it, but it was not there. He searched high and low but still there was no sign of it. With increasing anger, he realised that his foolish student had burnt his body without consulting him. He now had to find another body quickly and the only other recently dead body in the neighbourhood was that of the mishapen beggar. Ti Kuai Li reluctantly entered the beggar's body. As Ti Kuai Li painfully pulled himself to his feet he heard someone laughing. An old, white bearded man, carrying a bag of potions and herbs, was standing at the side of the road.

'Do you know me?' asked Ti Kuai Li.

'Of course I do,' replied the old man. 'Come here, come to me. Here is a bottle that contains a magic elixir which can help anyone and everyone. Your ugliness will frighten people but when they discover that you can cure any illness, the poor will call you to their homes and princes will summon you to their palaces.'

'But how much medicine is in the bottle?' asked Ti Kuai Li.

'Ah, this medicine is eternal. However much you need this bottle will produce.'

Ti Kuai Li stood before the old man. His body was bent and his leg was bleeding.

'You can't go far without a crutch,' said the old man.

Saying this, he shook the bottle and poured out some metal powder into the palm of his hand. He then poured some water from the gourd at his side and moulded the powder into a long metal rod. 'This crutch will never rust and never break. It will always be your support wherever you go and whatever you do.'

The old man handed Ti Kuai Li the crutch and the bottle. 'You are now ready to join the Immortals,' he said. 'You can go wherever you want. I am leaving you now.'

'But where are you going?' said Ti Kuai Li, overcome by this honour but frightened by his new responsibility.

'I am going to see Lao Tzu,' said the old man. 'This bottle was bestowed on you by Lao Tzu. I am merely his messenger and I must tell him.'

And at that the old man left. Ti Kuai Li gazed after him and knew that he had just spoken with Lao Tzu. With his new gift of immortality Ti Kuai Li travelled to many lands and could be found wherever the sick lay dying or the poor were persecuted.

The Student's Mother

After Ti Kuai Li had taken on the body of the beggar, he tried to find out what had happened to his student. He was very angry with him for having not only gone off when he should have stayed, but also for burning his body! In his anger he asked everyone he met whether they had seen a scruffy looking student. At last, he met an old man who said that such a person had gone hurrying by the day before. He had stopped briefly for a drink, but then had rushed on again.

Following the direction indicated by the old man, Ti Kuai Li travelled for two days until at last he came to the family village of his student. As he drew near, he realised that someone in the village had died. Drums were beating as a procession of weeping mourners and elders dressed in white passed by him. Quietly entering the village he asked who had died. When he realised it was his student's mother, he understood what had happened.

Now, the student had seen the old beggar come into the village, but had thought nothing of it. Little did he realise that it was his master. He was, therefore, shocked when the old, dirty beggar came into the house and made for the body of his mother.

'What are you doing?' he shouted as Ti Kuai Li lifted the dead woman's head. 'Stop this instant!'

But Ti Kuai Li ignored the youth and proceeded to tip the contents of a magical gourd into the mouth of the dead woman. The mourners were too astonished to say a word, let alone move. They stood with their mouths open, gaping at the strange sight.

Suddenly, the body shook. A deep cough came from the dead woman and her eyes opened! With a startled cry she leapt up and glared at Ti Kuai Li. 'What are you doing you dirty old beggar! How dare you disturb a sleeping woman.' Then she looked at the astonished mourners. 'What are you all staring at? And who has died in our village? I must find my mourning clothes.'

When they told her that it was she who had died, the poor woman fainted. When she came round, they explained what had happened. Now everyone turned their attention to Ti Kuai Li. 'Who are you?' they asked.

'My name is Ti Kuai Li,' he said and the student fainted on hearing these words. When they had brought him round, Ti Kuai Li explained everything. His student was horrified when he learnt what had happened and begged Ti Kuai Li's forgiveness.

'Don't apologise. You behaved like a good son towards your mother. I cannot blame you for that, but I cannot be your teacher now. You must follow the path yourself. But to help you, swallow this and in years to come, you will become an immortal.' He handed his student a little pill and as the student swallowed it, Ti Kuai Li disappeared in a swirling gust of wind.

Many many years later, Ti Kuai Li's promise was fulfilled and the student did become an immortal.

The Fragrant Nine
Crooked Stream

Anyone plying a bamboo raft or a rowing boat down the Nine Crooked Stream in Bohea will usually feel a soft, gentle wind against their skin and be enchanted by the view. The other thing they cannot fail to notice is the deliciously fragrant air. Some may tell you that it comes from the crops, others may say it is the scent of the cliff flowers, but they are wrong. The aroma comes from the wine flowing in the water. There is a story that reveals how this came to be.

In ancient times, an old farmer worked several fields bordering on the Nine Crooked Stream. As nobody knew his real name, they just called him Farm Father. He was a skilled brewer who stored his wine in a rough, hand-fashioned earthenware jar. When he uncorked the jar, an endless stream of fine wine flowed out – the wine that gave farmers enough energy to work for a year without feeling tired and gave travellers enough strength to walk nine thousand, nine hundred miles without feeling footsore. The old farmer's name, like his wine, was well-known everywhere.

The Eight Immortals had travelled to every corner of China, except Bohea and the day eventually came when they decided to make a visit. Tales of Farm Father's excellent wine had reached their ears and so a visit to his farm would be an extra bonus, particularly for Ti Kuai Li, a lover of good wine.

Ti Kuai Li could hardly wait to taste Farm Father's excellent brew and many a time he had told the others that they would regret being immortal unless they tasted this wine.

On the day of their departure, the Immortals changed into human form – four of them turned into tea merchants and four of them into Taoist priests. They flew high over rivers and mountains until they reached Farm Father's door. He welcomed them warmly as he always welcomed visiting friends and strangers. The earthenware jar was carefully lifted from a shelf by the open fireplace and eight clay bowls were filled to the rim. When the Immortals had emptied them, they were filled again to satisfy the Immortals unquenchable thirst. The jar did its duty and produced copious amounts of wine much to the Immortals' delight. The Immortals were completely charmed by its unusual delicate flavour and by evening three of the Immortals were dozing contentedly from its effects, while the other five raised their voices in a raucous song.

The Immortals had taken a strong liking to Bohea and particularly to Farm Father's house, so much so that they were loathe to leave after two weeks' holiday. Nevertheless, they had to leave to perform duites in other parts of China, but whenever they could they returned to Farm Father's house. Ti Kuai Li, particularly, formed a firm friendship with the old man, spending many happy hours drinking and talking with him, never failing to congratulate him on his fine wine. One day Ti Kuai Li asked the old man the secret of his wine-making.

'There is no secret,' replied the old man. 'I grow vines close to the rice fields, I take water from the Nine Crooked Stream and I store it in the earthenware jar that was fired in Yu Lin's furnace.'

Ti Kuai Li jumped to his feet excitedly. 'Then that is the answer,' he cried. 'It is the land and water of Bohea that gives it its unique taste. I hope this land never fails to yield such pleasing fruits.'

As Ti Kuai Li once again began an eulogy on Farm Father's fine wine, there was a heavy and impatient banging on the door. In his excitement Ti Kuai Li had forgotten P'an T'au's birthday party in heaven. It was the third day of the third lunar month and the seven other Immortals had come to collect him, suspecting that the party had slipped his memory. They pulled an unwilling Ti Kuai Li away from his bowl of wine, dragged him out of the farm house and then flew up into the heavens with him, keeping a tight grip on his arms and legs.

They landed as the party was in full swing. Gold tables were heavily laden with ripe immortal peaches, plums, melons and mangoes and endless rows of wine pitchers lined the walls. Ti Kuai Li was given a porcelain bowl filled with heavenly wine. He took one sip and had to force himself not to spit it out.

'What do you mean by giving me this,' he declared loudly.

The other Immortals tried to quieten him down but, there was no stopping him. He continued drunkenly, 'Bohea's wine is a hundred times more delicious and a thousand times more fragrant than this wine. I refuse to drink it.'

Ti Kuai Li soon attracted an amused crowd, all except for P'an T'au who was both angry and embarassed by Ti Kuai Li's criticisms. She immediately summoned her brewers and sent them with Ti Kuai Li to Bohea to find Farm Father and buy as much wine as he could spare. The old man was only too pleased to give his wine free of charge, as it was an honour to receive such a request from heaven.

While Ti Kuai Li stayed chatting and drinking with Farm Father, the brewers flew with the wine at the speed of lightning back to heaven. There the wine from Bohea was met with tumultuous acclaim by all the party guests who were soon in a magnificent state of euphoria. All except Ti Kuai Li, who, as usual, arrived late.

He wandered around the tables peering into bowls and jars, but they were empty. He looked under the tables and rummaged amongst the food but there wasn't a drop of wine to be found. In anger, Ti Kuai Li grabbed the chief brewer, raised his staff into the air and brought it down with a hard thump. Unfortunately, the wine he had drunk had impaired his vision. His staff missed the brewer by more than a hand's length and landed like a bag of stones on one of Farm Father's precious earthenware jars that the brewer was holding, forming a thin crack from the neck to the base. The jar fell from the brewer's hands, rolled across the palace floor, out of the doorway, out of heaven and down to earth. Luckily, it landed on the south side of the Nine Crooked Stream in Bohea and there it stayed for hundreds of years. The jar eventually grew into a craggy peak, known as the Heaven Pole Peak, but a small trickle of wine continued to leak from the hairline crack. The wine still trickles into the waters of the Nine Crooked Stream to this day and this is why the air in Bohea is so fragrant.

The Eight Immortals' Table

Hsiao Neng Jen was born and brought up in the village of Wild Tiger Camp in Hupeh province. He had great aspirations to immortality but loathed study and effort. He despised work and believed that immortality could help him further his passion for food and wine. And so Hsiao Neng Jen spent endless days and nights dreaming of immortality. He awoke abruptly one morning with severe hunger pangs so he dragged himself out of bed and stumbled out of the house intent on stealing sweetcorn from a neighbour's fields.

He couldn't believe his eyes when he arrived at a nearby farm. The Eight Immortals were sitting on a stone table underneath a willow, their faces lit by the flickering shadows of an oil lamp.

At first the Immortals were unaware of this stranger, and secure in their privacy, they discussed the day's work. Suddenly, the oil lamp began to spark, a warning that a human was nearby. The Immortals stood up quickly and noiselessly and disappeared into the darkness, all except Ti Kuai Li. He tried to hobble away quickly but his deformed leg slowed him down and before he could disappear, Hsiao Neng Jen blocked his path.

'Ti Kuai Li, great Immortal, please don't go away,' pleaded Hsiao Neng Jen. 'Night after night I have dreamt of you sitting beside me, guiding me and teaching me. I beg you with all my heart, help me become immortal. I will do anything you ask to prove my worth.'

Ti Kuai Li closed his eyes in thought. He had heard admirable stories of a worthy student living in Wild Tiger Camp and thought that this must be the student. But before Ti Kuai Li could utter a word, Hsiao Neng Jen fell to his feet and saluted Ti Kuai Li as a student would to a master.

'Hold on young man,' said Ti Kuai Li sternly. 'To prove your worth as a student, you have to do something which other humans would not be prepared to do.'

'Oh, I can do anything you ask,' replied Hsiao Neng Jen confidently. 'Even if you asked me to eat dung I would do it.'

'That is a good reply,' complimented Ti Kuai Li, as he turned in the direction of the stream. 'Can you see that cow pat over there, on the stream's muddy banks?'

The student nodded, secretly afraid that he would have to prove his boast.

'Go down to the stream,' continued Ti Kuai Li. 'I command you to eat that cow pat. Once you have swallowed it, we can travel together to heaven.'

This was more than Hsiao Neng Jen had expected, but he thought it was a small price to pay for the pleasures of immortality. He knelt down beside the stream but didn't attempt to touch the cow pat.

'Go on,' urged Ti Kuai Li. 'You must do this before the first light of day or else you will never see me again.'

Hsiao Neng Jen unwillingly took some of the cow pat into his hand, but he was so repulsed by the look and the smell that he vomited into the stream. He could hear Ti Kuai Li's voice continually urging him on, but he felt dizzy and faint. A sweat broke out on his forehead, his hands trembled and his stomach turned over and over. He could hear Ti Kuai Li's voice becoming more and more faint.

'The dawn is on its way Hsiao Neng Jen. If you cannot fulfil one simple order, how can you expect the gift of immortality. This opportunity will never come again. I am leaving you now. I am leaving you.'

Ti Kuai Li's voice trailed off into the darkness just as Hsiao Neng Jen slumped to the ground in grief.

'Please, please, don't go, don't abandon me,' he sobbed.

But it was too late, T'i Kuai Li had gone from his life forever.

The sound of a cock crowing pulled Hsiao Neng Jen out of his stupor and he stumbled back home. He immediately ordered his wife to fetch a bowl of water to wash the unbearable smell from his hands. But no sooner had he put his hands in the water than the smell of orchids in full bloom filled the air. Hsiao Neng Jen upturned the bowl of water, pushed his wife aside and raced down to the muddy stream. Now he had the strength to eat the cow dung, but there was nothing by the stream except brown, slimy mud.

Hsiao Neng Jen sank his head into his hands and wept and wept. When he felt as though every emotion had been drained from his body, he crept underneath the stone table where the Immortals had sat and fell asleep. When he awoke he refused food and water from his distraught wife. He just lay there waiting for the Immortals to return. But Hsiao Neng Jen never saw the Eight Immortals again. He died underneath the stone table and his body turned to stone. To this day his stone shape can be seen underneath the 'Eight Immortals' Table', just outside the village of Wild Tiger Camp.

The Punishment of K'uang Tzu Lien

The Eight Immortals met regularly at the Immortals' Bridge to discuss what they had seen and heard on their travels. One afternoon they sat on the small arched stone bridge singing folk songs until darkness fell and then Chang Kuo Lao called for silence. He stood up before his attentive friends to reveal news of a dispute in a distant province.

'Fifteen miles from Man Yo street, there is a large stone house with a heavy alabaster door. It is the home of K'uang Tzu Lien, a wealthy farmer and merchant. He owns ten thousand acres of rich farming lands not to mention numerous fine houses and chests of jewel-encrusted silver and gold. It would take fifteen strong men just to carry these chests. But he has become wealthy at the expense of the poor farmers who work his lands and the underpaid labourers who build his houses. I have heard that he will be sixty years old in a few days and plans to throw a huge party. At this very moment he is making preparations for his guests. In order to prove his wealth he has filled the holes in the road with rice and laid a pure red woollen carpet over this smooth surface.

The Eight Immortals listened in stunned silence until Ti Kuai Li interrupted angrily, 'How dare he waste grain which can feed hundreds of people and what right does he have to waste pure wool which can clothe the needy. He is using grain and wool like dirt for the rich to walk upon. I have heard enough, I am going to teach him a lesson.'

As he stood up, he changed his gourd hanging from his waist into a begging bowl. Using his gift of flight, Ti Kuai Li arrived in a few seconds at K'uang Tzu Lien's opulent house. Delicately carved wooden beams supported the roof, dragons and phoenix were painted in gold on the walls and the front door was made of pure white alabaster. Servants were busy brushing the red woollen carpet, polishing the marble pillars, and carrying baskets laden with the finest produce of the land and of the sea. Other servants were clambering to attend to the needs of the stream of guests arriving by sedan chair. House servants, dressed in black and gold embroidered clothes, were setting hand painted porcelain dishes and ivory chopsticks upon the red lacquered chairs and tables.

Ti Kuai Li could feel a soft crinching noise beneath his feet and lifting the red carpet he saw a bed of rice six inches thick.

'So the story is true,' he thought. 'This man has wasted enough rice to feed the local people for a year.'

More than a hundred beggars stood silently on either side of the carpet, their faces wracked with hunger and anger. Ti Kuai Li approached the marble door of the house, but was halted by five servants who demanded angrily, 'Old beggar, what are you doing here? Stand back in the dirt where you belong.'

Ti Kuai Li stood his ground and calmly questioned them, 'I understand that your master is holding a party. I beg you to give me some of the leftover food.'

The house servants laughed scornfully at the old beggar. 'Our master would rather send the leftovers to the pigs or put them in a dustbin than feed them to a dirty beggar. We don't want you here upsetting the enjoyment of our honoured guests.'

On saying this the guards stepped forward and struck Ti Kuai Li about the face and head. Ti Kuai Li reeled back, his nose and mouth covered in blood. As he struggled to his feet he tried to pick up a handful of rice but the guards seized his wrists and forced him to drop it. But Ti Kuai Li was not so easily defeated and continued to plead with the guards. 'You have strewn a thousand shih worth of rice on the road. Please, I beg you, allow me to collect a bowlful to feed my ageing parents and my hungry children.'

But the servants stopped him once again saying, 'Our master would rather have it ground underfoot to powder than give it to the beggars who are destroying the pleasure of our party.'

'The rich should beware of cheating the needy and insulting the poor,' replied Ti Kuai Li with authority.

The servants were enraged at this reply. 'You dirty good-for-nothing! How dare you criticise or try to teach our master.'

They kicked Ti Kuai Li to the floor and continued to beat him viciously until he could no longer move. They then strode back to the marble entrance. The other beggars who had seen Ti Kuai Li's courage and determination, now rushed to his side and pleaded with him, 'Good friend, you must return home. They are rich and powerful people who will kill you without thinking twice.'

But Ti Kuai Li was not to be overcome and vowed in a coarse, weak voice, 'I will teach them even if they have to kill me.'

Meanwhile sounds of feasting could be heard from inside the house. A hundred tables were groaning beneath the weight of freshly caught fish, roasted suckling pigs, dishes piled high with prawns and crabs, trays of ducks and chickens, pans of rice and noodles and baskets of ripe fruit. The wealthiest aristocrats and merchants sat on the top table with K'uang Tzu Lien. Their bowls were continually filled with delicacies and their glasses were brimming with the best wine. Then, without warning, the bowls on the top table began to heat up. The porcelain became so hot that the servants dropped them on the floor and the guests let them fall from their mouths. Trying to be polite towards their host, the guests continued to eat with the ivory chopsticks, but before their very eyes their food became infested with maggots.

The maggots crawled from the pig's flesh, out of the noodles and amongst the fish lying on golden trays. Everyone drew back from the table in horror and K'uang Tzu Lien, his face purple with anger and embarrassment, ran to the head chef in the kitchens.

'Clear the tables,' he demanded breathlessly as he hit the chef across the face. 'Bring new dishes immediately. How dare you shame me in front of my friends.'

No sooner had the servants brought fresh sweet-smelling dishes into the hall, than the guests on the top table began to scream, 'There are maggots in the soup. You have given us bowls of maggots instead of bowls of rice. The pitchers of wine are full of maggots. Thousands of maggots are writhing beneath the skin of the ducks and chickens.'

The other guests were drawn to the scene at the top table and gathered round in surprise and shock, whispering to one another, 'K'uang Tzu Lien has played a foolish trick. He will never be forgiven. No one will ever come to his table again.'

At one moment K'uang Tzu Lien's face was red with anger, at another white with shock. 'I know the devil who has done this,' he declared venomously. 'It is the impudent old beggar my guards told me about. I have heard that beggars sometimes have the power to turn food to maggots.'

He called his guards to the table. 'Come with me. I am going to teach this beggar a lesson he will never forget.'

They ran to the doorway where the beggars were huddled around Ti Kuai Li. The guards pushed the beggars aside and dragged Ti Kuai Li across the floor and laid him at the feet of K'uang Tzu Lien who demanded harshly, 'Who are you? Where have you come from?'

'I am only a poor beggar,' replied Ti Kuai Li modestly. 'I heard of your lavish party and have walked miles to beg for leftover food at your door. Your guards have beaten me for making this request and now you can see my bruised bleeding face.'

Ti Kuai Li's body then shook violently as he vomited blood and after a few seconds he lay motionless before the stunned crowd.

'What are you looking at?' demanded K'uang Tzu Lien. 'It is only a beggar. Wrap his body in a mat and bury him under the mud.'

K'uang Tzu Lien returned to his guests, leaving the guards to bury Ti Kuai Li. But the beggars who had witnessed the murder ran to see Chao Shen Chiao, the just police commissioner, in the nearby town of Hunan and recounted the story while he listened attentively.

'I have heard that K'uang Tzu Lien was mad,' he said, 'and this story only confirms my suspicions. He thinks he can buy protection but a wealthy man is never outside the law. Guards, prepare my sedan chair immediately. We are going to K'uang Tzu Lien's estate.'

As they approached the house, the police saw a crowd of people milling outside the marble door. K'uang Tzu Lien's servants had tried to move the body but not even five of his strongest men could lift the dead man's hand. Even K'uang Tzu himself, drawn by the commotion outside, had tried to move the beggar but had failed. It was only then that he had realised that this was no ordinary beggar. As he discussed the problem with his servants he heard his guard announce, 'Make way for the old gentleman of Hunan.'

The crowd pulled aside and knelt down to welcome Chao Shen Chiao, but without saying a word to K'uang Tzu Lien the commissioner knelt down beside Ti Kuai Li's body. He called for a Taoist teacher in the crowd and a man in a red robe stepped forward.

'Could you plase examine him,' asked Chao Shen Chiao. 'Tell me if there is anything unusual.'

The teacher walked slowly around the body and bent down to examine Ti Kuai Li's pockets. He drew a piece of brown rice paper from Ti Kuai Ti's torn cotton jacket. The crowd was hushed as the teacher read out loud the words written on it.

'I do not want K'uang Tzu Lien to pay for this crime with his life. I want him to sweep the roads leading from his house to every town and village in this province. He must learn that a rich man cannot cheat the poor.'

Chao Shen Chiao grabbed the rice paper from the teacher and read the words again and again until it finally dawned on him who this beggar really was. He bellowed to his guards, 'Arrest K'uang Tzu Lien. Bring him before me.'

The guards did as they were commanded and K'uang Tzu Lien was forced to kneel at the commissioner's feet.

'You have murdered one of the Eight Immortals,' accused Chao Shen Chiao. 'You are the murderer of Ti Kuai Li. Are you going to pay for your crime with your life or with your money?'

'Take my land, take my jewels, take anything but my life,' cried K'uang Tzu Lien.

'As you wish,' said Chao Shen Chiao. 'Your lands, houses and jewels are now public property. Your remaining days will be spent sweeping the dirt from the roads. Guards, chain him up and take him away.'

K'uang Tzu Lien was lead through a jeering and jostling crowd. Meanwhile the beggars once more tried to lift Ti Kuai Li's body and this time it was as light as a feather. They carried it across the red woollen carpet to a place of rest underneath a nearby tree, but Chao Shen Chiao ordered a full inquiry before the burial could take place.

Several weeks later, permission was given to bury the body. The whole town turned out for the burial but when the most respected members of the town lifted the coffin to their shoulders, it was as light as air. They rested the coffin on the floor and prized open the lid. The coffin was empty! Filled with fear and anxiety, they rushed to Chao Shen Chiao's office and demanded an investigation but the wise commissioner sent a message through his chief.

'Tell the townspeople not to worry. It is only Ti Kuai Li's body that has disappeared. His spirit will never leave us. Whenever we need him, he will be there to help us.'

The commissioner was right. After Ti Kuai Li had been placed in the coffin his body has changed to smoke and risen to the sky. He had returned to the Immortals' Bridge where the other Immortals were still talking and singing.

The Black Pearl

The two fishermen lived in adjoining cottages near a bridge spanning the Yangtze river. One always woke at noon and passed several lazy hours fishing on the river. The other rose at dawn and spent all day fishing. Naturally his catch was always greater than the lazy fisherman's, but nevertheless he helped him when he needed food or money. For some reason the fish that they caught never survived outside the fast flowing waters of the Yangtze. Although they immediately put their catch into buckets of water, the fish died within minutes. The shoppers at the market only bought their fish as a last choice and even the hardworking fisherman found it difficult to make a living.

One night the hardworking fisherman had a vivid dream which changed his life forever. He dreamt that a white bearded old man approached him as he was mending nets one evening outside his cottage.

'Good evening fisherman,' the old man said. 'Your fortune will soon change for the better. Tomorrow morning, before dawn, the Eight Immortals will cross the bridge near your cottage. Wait there for them. If you recognise any one of them, stop him and ask for a precious gift. Don't be afraid to speak to them, they are there to help you. If you do what I say, your fortune will change forever.'

When he woke up, the fisherman didn't know whether to believe this dream or not, but he decided to wait by the bridge in case it had been true. Just before dawn he spotted a group of people dressed in old fashioned robes coming over the hump of the bridge. They walked slowly, chatting pleasantly to one another, completely unaware that they were being watched. The fisherman stared at them intently but didn't recognise any of them. He was about to give up hope and return home, when he suddenly caught sight of a bent figure hobbling towards him. His face was pock marked and ugly, a corked gourd hung from his leather belt and he walked with the aid of an iron staff. At last the fisherman recognised one of the Immortals and he ran forward calling his name excitedly.

'Ti Kuai Li, Ti Kuai Li. I have been told that you will give me a precious gift. I am sorry to stop you so unexpectedly but is this true?'

inquired the fisherman, trying hard not to sound too demanding or too eager.

Ti Kuai Li slowly looked at the fisherman from head to foot. He saw his battered straw sandals, his threadbare clothes, his calloused hands and his honest, weather-beaten face. He knew instinctively that the fisherman was generous and dedicated to his work and would undoubtedly use a gift from an Immortal wisely. Ti Kuai Li unplugged his gourd, tipped it slightly and out rolled a smooth, black glossy pearl. He then handed the pearl to the fisherman, told him how to use it and advised him to keep it in a safe place, away from prying eyes and careless hands. Ti Kuai Li patted the fisherman on the back and disappeared just as the first cockcrow greeted the dawn.

From that day the fisherman caught the usual amount of fish, put them in a bucket of water and sold them the next day. But his fish were not only alive when they reached the market, they were also larger than the fish on other stalls. Each day, long queues of eager buyers lined up beside his buckets of fish and before long the fisherman had amassed a small fortune. Meanwhile, the lazy fisherman grew suspicious and jealous. He knew from experience that the fish in the Yangtze were small and limited in variety, so how did his neighbour manage to catch fish of all shapes and sizes? Furthermore, how did he manage to keep his fish alive overnight?

The jealous fisherman suspected his prosperous neighbour of sorcery or magic and so he decided to follow his movements. Instead of going to bed at sunset, as he usually did, the lazy fisherman crept under cover of darkness through his neighbour's garden and settled himself by a narrow crack in the back door. The room was brightly lit by two oil lamps and he could see everything that happened. The industrious fisherman emptied a sackful of freshly caught dead fish into a bucket full of water. Then he carefully took a black pearl out of a straw purse hanging around his neck and held the pearl on the water's surface for ten seconds. At once the dead fish came to life, slapping their tales against the bucket and pushing one another for swimming space. The small plain-looking fish were transformed into huge colourful and unusual fish. The lazy fisherman couldn't stand the suspense any longer and burst impatiently into the room.

'Now I know why you make so much money,' he shouted, but calmed down quickly before he made his plaintive request. 'We have been friends for many years so you know how poor I am. Please lend me the pearl for two nights and I promise to return it.'

The industrious fisherman put the pearl on the table beside him. Ti

Good Luck and Good Fish (from an early 20th-century Chinese design)

Kuai Li had ordered him not to lend the pearl to anyone no matter how hard they begged, but the industrious fisherman could not leave a friend in trouble. He promised to take him to the bridge to meet Ti Kuai Li. If anyone could help this lazy fisherman, the great Immortal could. But the lazy fisherman had no time for promises, all he wanted was the pearl. While the industrious fisherman was talking, his greedy neighbour could not take his eyes off this magic gift and eventually his patience ran out and he lunged for the pearl.

The industrious fisherman grabbed it just in time and had no choice but to swallow it. At that very moment thunder rolled across the sky making the cottage walls shudder. The cottage roof was ripped off by a streak of lightning and the furniture was thrown aside. The lazy fisherman cowered fearfully in a corner but the industrious fisherman stood motionless in the middle of the room, until another streak of lightning hit his body. But instead of being thrown to the floor he rose slowly towards heaven. He soon disappeared into the star-filled sky where he joined the gods and the immortals. When the lazy fisherman plucked up the courage to leave the ruined cottage he headed straight for the bridge hoping to catch Ti Kuai Li, but he didn't appear that night nor did he appear on the following twenty nights. The lazy fisherman didn't have the patience to wait any longer and returned to his usual habit of rising at noon. He had pushed his friend's generosity too far and he died as he had lived, in poverty.

The Lame Healer

The old man who lived beside the stone bridge in Hangchow was a healer of abscesses, boils and lameness. The local people doubted his powers but came to visit him nevertheless.

A thick black beard concealed the lower half of his face. His dark eyes peered out from bushy eyebrows which met in the middle of a wide forehead. As long as the villagers could remember he had been lame. He supported himself with a roughly beaten metal staff and a gourd containing medicine was permanently thrown across his shoulder.

Each day, regardless of the weather, he lay his medicines and plasters on a well-used wooden chest shaded by a black and red cotton and bamboo umbrella. Each night he stowed the medicine in the wooden chest, unrolled a straw mat on top of the box and slept there till the first light of dawn. He never changed his routine and after several years, nobody had bothered to count, he had become a familiar and accepted sight in the town.

One spring morning he was visited by a man who had been lame for three years after an accident in a stonemason's workshop. The condition of his leg had slowly deteriorated so he finally decided to try his luck with the lame healer. After a brief consultation the healer rummaged in his chest and pulled out a large paper and herb plaster that he commonly called a 'dog skin plaster'. He handed this to the lame man saying, 'Leave this on your leg for at least three days and if you have any problems return to me.'

The lame man did as he was told, but he had no need to return as his leg healed completely. Word of the miraculous cure spread quickly and within a week, people of the village formed queues to consult the healer who sat under the shade of the black and red umbrella giving out advice and 'dog skin plasters'.

The man who had once been scorned by the people of Hang-chow was now a popular talking point. He was given a name, Sai Hua To, a name which recalled the immortal Hua To, a skilled healer.

But his fame also aroused jealousy amongst the town's herbalists, acupuncturists and healers, since their once thriving businesses

Shen-Nung, God of Medicine (from a late 19th-century Chinese woodcut)

were now wasting from Sai Hua To's popular practice. His jealous competitors held a secret meeting to try and find a way to ruin Sai Hua To's reputation. After hours of debate they reached a decision and immediately sent two representatives to Chih Fu, the chief administrator of the prefecture. In a dimly lit room at the back of Chih Fu's house the representatives handed over a thousand coins as a bribe for the arrest of Sai Hua To.

That same night, guards were sent to arrest Sai Hua To. They awoke him roughly, pulled him off the wooden chest, handcuffed him and led him to the cells in the prefectural building. Early the following morning the innocent Sai Hua To was taken into Chih Fu's office for questioning. Chih Fu rapped the table with a ruler demanding silence.

'Kneel before me, healer. Show respect to your superiors.'

Sai Hua To answered meekly, 'You will have to forgive me. I am a lame man, unable to kneel down. My bones are twisted and my leg is stiff.'

Chih Fu rapped the table once again, demanding angrily, 'Who are you, where do you come from?'

'I've never had a real name but most people call me Sai Hua To. As to where I come from, I am sorry, but I can't tell you because I can't remember,' the healer replied humbly, eyes lowered before his furious interrogator.

Chih Fu lowered his gaze to Sai Hua To's lame leg. 'If you are so skilled, why don't you heal your own lameness?' he said mockingly.

As he spoke, Chih Fu felt an itch across his back as though an insect was crawling underneath his cotton jacket. He scratched himself but there was nothing there. Up to now Sai Hua To had watched and listened quietly and respectfully, but now he could contain himself no longer and burst out laughing.

'Your honour, you may be a clever man, but if you'll excuse me saying this, you are being extremely stupid at the moment. You have asked a healer why he can't heal himself. Look around your prefecture, look around the province. There are businesses everywhere that help other people yet they cannot help themselves. Labourers can build palaces for others but they still live in hovels. Silk merchants sell delicate embroidered silks but wear cotton clothes. Farmers grow cartloads of grain but are sometimes too weak from hunger to farm their fields. You arrest thieves who know right from wrong and have still committed a crime.'

Chih Fu was left speechless with anger after this outburst. His face grew purple with rage and finally he bellowed out an order to his deputy. 'Take this man away. Lock him in a cell on death row.'

Having passed sentence, Chih Fu returned to his house in a fierce temper. As he sat down for a meal, he felt a severe itch on his back but this time it did not fade. After removing his jacket he ordered his servant to examine his back. There was nothing but a small patch of hard skin, but as the day wore on the itch became more painful and the patch of hard skin grew and grew. By dinner time, the hard skin covered a quarter of Chih Fu's back and by bedtime, the skin had erupted into a hard inflamed boil. With a painful cry, Chih Fu called for his servant to help him.

'Master, I think there is someone who can help you,' said the servant. 'Why not ask the old lame healer who lives by the bridge. He will be able to help you before he is beheaded.'

Unable to bear his suffering any longer, Chih Fu gave Sai Hua To permission to visit him at home. Late at night, Sai Hua To was brought handcuffed to Chih Fu's house by two guards. After examining the boil intently the healer offered Chih Fu a 'dog skin plaster'. Chih Fu accepted the plaster without gratitude and ordered Sai Hua To back to his cell.

Chih Fu passed the following day in pain and misery and by evening his suffering was so intense he was unable to move. The boil was filled with pus and bleeding continuously. Its acrid stench could even be smelt through three closed doors. Not even Chih Fu's wife dared approach him for fear of fainting or contagion. By dawn Chih Fu was helpless and in anger and exasperation he once more ordered the guards to bring the lame healer to his home. Sai Hua To was accordingly led before the furious prefect. 'Look at me healer,' he cried. 'I have never felt such bad pain in my life. You have tried to poison me with your plaster. I should have killed you the moment I laid eyes on you.'

'Hold on,' replied Sai Hua To. 'Before you blame me for your agony, let me examine your boil.' Sai Hua To carefully peeled back the plaster and examined the boil.

'The head of the boil is small but the swelling is great,' he declared. 'You are festering inside and the badness in your heart has erupted on the surface of the skin. There is nothing I can do to help you. Your unkindness and cruelty, not my plaster, has made you suffer.'

After hearing Sai Hua To's diagnosis, Chih Fu was filled with fear. He picked up a clay water jug at the side of his bed and threw it at the healer, screaming, 'Get him out! Get this wretch out of my sight! Behead him immediately, show him no mercy!'

No sooner had he said this, when his body convulsed with spasm, his breathing became harsh and heavy and his eyes rolled up into his sockets. Chih Fu took one final breath and collapsed dead on his bed.

The guards carried out their master's final command. Sai Hua To was charged with sorcery and bound in chains. That same day he was led through the streets of Hangchow to the punishment block and as he passed by the stone bridge that was his home the local people crowded round loudly proclaiming his innocence. Sai Hua To raised his chained hands to quieten them, saying, 'My friends, listen to me. The prefect is forcing me to go to heaven. I am not yet ready so I go unwillingly.'

And then, before the guards could react, Sai Hua To threw himself off the bridge into the turbulent waters below. As he hit the water a cloud of green smoke rose to the sky. The shocked crowd gasped and the smoke parted to reveal Sai Hua To ascending to the heavens carrying his gourd and metal staff. Their gaze followed him until he disappeared from view in the clouds. It was only then that they realised that the lame healer, who had been living amongst them for so long, was Ti Kuai Li, one of the Eight Immortals.

To this day, people throughout China remember Ti Kuai Li's healing powers and, at festival time, they gather round the small stone bridge in Hangchow to pray for good health.

Donkey Fire

One day the Eight Immortals decided to visit P'eng Lang ('Fairy Town' – the traditional name for Peking). After a busy day visiting the temples and palaces, they made their way home on foot, except for Chang Kuo Lau who always travelled by donkey. The other Immortals walked home briskly but Chang Kuo Lau's donkey was exhausted after a busy day bearing his master from temple to temple. The donkey plodded along the road while the other Immortals disappeared from view, but neither Chang Kuo Lau or his donkey were perturbed. They would make it home eventually. The first evening stars had appeared when they stopped for a rest against the coral encrusted walls of the Sea Dragon's palace, unaware that they were being watched from the shadows by the wily Sea Crab King.

This was the opportunity that the Sea Crab King had been impatiently waiting for for more than two years. Hua Lung, a prince of the Eastern Sea, had fallen deeply in love with Ho Hsien Ku, the beautiful Immortal. He knew the only way to capture her would be to kidnap one of the Eight Immortals and hold him to ransom. The scheming Sea Crab King had been put in charge of the kidnapping and now he had the perfect opportunity. The Sea Crab King scuttled off to the shore to mobilise his troops for battle. With a piercing cry, he summoned crabs of all shapes and sizes – stream crabs, river crabs, lake crabs and sea crabs. On hearing the call, the crabs rushed furiously to their commander and assembled in tight lines close to the Sea Dragon's palace.

After a pleasant rest Chang Kuo Lau mounted his donkey and headed off in the direction of the Eastern Sea where the crabs waited in ambush. Chang Kuo Lau sang a song which carried clearly across the eerie darkness. Every now and then, he broke his tune to offer encouraging words to his donkey.

Then suddenly, as he rounded a sharp bend in the road, ten thousand pairs of piercing eyes glowed in the darkness. A mighty screech resounded through the night and thousands of crabs charged at him from every direction, squealing, scuttling, pushing, biting and scratching. They rushed in like a huge wave engulfing Chang Kuo Lau and his donkey. The petrified donkey kicked wildly, trampling many crabs underfoot, but he was weak against the crabs' vicious pincers which lacerated his legs. Chang Kuo Lau screamed for help to the other Immortals but his voice was drowned in the thundering clamour. The donkey knew that his master was in deadly danger and he had no choice but to use the secret weapon his master had bestowed on him. Chang Kuo Lau slapped the donkey three times on his rump and the donkey emitted a deafening roar which made the mountains tremble and the waves lash against the shore. At the same time, a jet of scorching fire streamed from the donkey's mouth. The wild flames leapt across the screaming crabs and the sea turned to fire. The crabs tumbled over one another in their rush to escape, but it was too late – they were burned to death. Their bright red bodies were strewn along the road and littered across the shore.

Ever since, crabs have been frightened of fire and if they are cooked they turn bright red in memory of that day.

A Thonged Straw Sandal

Chang Kuo Lau was born into a poor family who barely had enough money to support him. At the age of twelve he was forced to seek employment with a local farmer, a cruel and harsh man, nicknamed Ho Yen Wang by the locals.

Ho Yen Wang made the young boy work twice as hard as his own family, but gave him half the amount of food that he gave to his own son. Months rolled into years and Chang Kuo Lau was forced to follow the same gruelling routine. He rose before dawn to feed and milk the cattle and clean the pigstys. After breakfast, the house had to be cleaned, the wood collected and chopped, the farmyard swept, eggs collected and seeds planted or crops harvested. Apart from stopping for a meagre evening meal, Chang Kuo Lau was not allowed to rest until midnight. At New Year, when all the other boys were free to play, Chang Kuo Lau could be found scrubbing the floors or feeding the animals.

The time came when the farmer no longer needed the boy. He was too old to live as part of their family and furthermore he required too much food. One day the farmer approached Chang Kuo Lau and put his arm around the boy's shoulder, as though he was offering him wise advice.

'My dear brother, you are now old enough to start a family of your own. As a token of my gratitude you must take this donkey.'

And behind the farmer, tethered to a wooden post, stood an old underfed and overworked donkey. Its legs were weak and spindly and its skin was wrapped tightly around its angular bones. Chang Kuo Lau had no choice but to accept the gift and leave his adopted home.

Chang Kuo Lau travelled the province with his donkey, usually sleeping rough by river banks or in tumbledown farm buildings. He scraped together money to survive by collecting wood from the mountains to sell in the towns. The boy grew to dread his journeys into the rocky mountains where his feet were torn by thorns and ripped by sharp stones. When he was finally unable to bear the pain any more he hit upon a clever solution. He gathered enough straw to wrap around his feet to protect them but these straw sandals soon fell apart. Chang Kuo Lau was not deterred. Each day he practised new ways of making straw sandals. He taught himself how to weave the straw tightly enough to withstand wear and tear and eventually developed a woven straw shoe that could protect his feet completely.

One autumn day when Chang Kuo Lau was selling firewood, he met Ho Yen Wang taking his poultry to market. The wily farmer had heard about Chang Kuo Lau's durable straw shoes and had decided to use the boy's skill to his advantage. He would pay Chang Kuo Lau a small sum to make the shoes and then sell them to the barefoot farmers and peasants for a large profit. Chang Kuo Lau was therefore invited to a sumptuous meal in his old home. Instead of waiting at the table he was to be the centre of attention. After offering Chang Kuo Lau his choice of succulent dishes the farmer tentatively made his proposition.

'My dear brother, you and I have known some happy times together and I feel that we have been apart too long. Searching the mountains for firewood has made you old before your time. Why not return to my home to make straw shoes? I will give you ten ounces of silver as a yearly salary.'

But Chang Kuo Lau as not to be fooled again by the farmer's cunning tricks and politely declined. The farmer grew agitated.

'Well, what would you say if I offered you twenty ounces of silver?'

Chang Kuo Lau declined once again and so the farmer desperately continued to increase his offer. After half an hour of bargaining, Chang Kuo Lau finally lost his temper. He slammed his tea bowl on the table and jumped to his feet, overturning his chair and the other bowls on the table. He turned on Ho Yen Wang, his face scarlet with anger. 'I've had enough of your sly devious ways, old man. Even if you offered me all the silver in China I wouldn't touch your dirty money.'

Ho Yen Wang was furious at this unexpected outburst. He grabbed a walking stick that lay on the floor beneath the kitchen table, upturning the table in his haste, raised the stick high above his head and raised vicious blows on Chang Kuo Lau's feeble body. Ho Yen Wang was oblivious to Chang Kuo Lau's screams of pain and continued to beat his hunched body until he dropped the stick from sheer exhaustion. It was a still night and neighbouring farmers who had heard the commotion, came running into the kitchen.

They tenderly lifted Chang Kuo Lau into their arms and carried him to safety. Chang Kuo Lau had given them straw shoes as gifts when they were in need and now they could repay him. But Chang Kuo Lau knew that he would never recover. Many people came to visit him and amongst them he met Pai Nien, a young, earnest and trustworthy peasant boy.

One evening, when they were alone, Chang Kuo Lau confided in the boy. 'Pai Nien, I am too ill to make straw shoes for the poor people. I would like to teach you this skill and when I die you can carry on my work.'

Pai Nien was overjoyed to be chosen by a man who had won the respect of so many people and that same evening he began his lessons. Chang Kuo Lau's health deteriorated quickly. He had taught his student how to weave soles and make straw thongs but he lost the use of his hands before he could teach him how to make straw uppers. Not long after he lost the use of his hands, Chang Kuo Lau died. Pai Nien continued his master's tradition but unfortunately he could only make thonged straw sandals. He did not have the skill to make proper shoes. This is why farmers today wear straw sandals, but never straw shoes.

Why Chang Kuo Lau Rides His Donkey Backwards

There is another story about Chang Kuo Lau's early life. Chang Kuo Lau's family scratched a meagre living from their small plot of land. The family ate once a day and the rest of the farm's produce was sold to the local people and so the family raised enough money to buy new seeds and repair their farm. It was Chang Kuo Lau's duty to deliver fruit and vegetables riding on the back of a donkey. He had done this job since he could remember and by now had established a familiar route. Each day, at midday, he stopped in an abandoned and secluded temple to eat a simple lunch and have an hour's sleep. Chang Kuo Lau usually woke up refreshed from his sleep, but one day he woke up still feeling weak and hungry. A delicious aroma wafted through the collapsed doorway of the temple. It filled every corner of the room where he lay and increased his appetite to such an extent that he doubled up with hunger pains. He instantly forgot all about his deliveries for that day and went in search of the source of this wonderful smell. He stumbled across the weeds and stones strewn across the temple floor and grew increasingly ravenous with each step. He searched each corner of the temple and finally, tucked out of sight in an overgrown corner of the courtyard, he spotted a huge pan of simmering food. Chang Kuo Lau looked around cautiously to see if there was anyone watching him. It was strange to find a pan of mouthwatering food without an owner, but he had already searched the temple and it had been empty. Unable to resist the temptation any longer, he made a pair of impromptu chopsticks from nearby reeds and dipped them into the pan. The food was delicious, the most satisfying and nourishing meal he had ever tasted and so he couldn't resist helping himself to another portion. This was even more satisfying than the first mouthful and only served to whet his unsatiable appetite. Chang Kuo Lau could not help himself. He just had to eat more and so he knelt down by the pan and started to devour the food eagerly.

But the pan was not a gift from the gods. It had been left there for a purpose. A local teacher, a devout student of Taoism, had discovered the location of a rare herb, a herb that would give him immortality. Under cover of darkness he dug up the herb and took it to the deserted temple and by the first light of dawn he had chopped the herb into small pieces and set it simmering in the pan under a tray of charcoal. He planned to sneak into the temple after school to eat everything in the pan. The teacher was on tenterhooks all day and could barely speak to the children because he was so excited about his imminent release from this life. As the last pupil filed from the classroom, he checked to see if anyone was watching him and ran home as quickly as he could to collect a bowl and chopsticks.

Unfortunately a good friend was waiting for him when he arrived home. 'Could you please do me the honour of coming to my party,' he asked earnestly. 'I have a set of red scrolls which need to be inscribed and your expert calligraphy would look so good on them.'

The teacher could hardly refuse his friend's request and set off with him to the party. Determined to keep his secret safe, the teacher impatiently illustrated the scrolls and excused himself from the party with a severe headache. Finally he was free and dashed to the temple completely unaware that Chang Kuo Lau was happily finishing off the last morsels of his precious herb. Every now and then Chang Kuo Lau gave his donkey a mouthful of this delicious stew, so by the time the teacher arrived the donkey and his master were sitting contentedly by an empty pan oblivious to the teacher who stood dumbfounded in the doorway. As Chang Kuo Lau lazily moved himself to find a more comfortable position, he caught sight of the distraught teacher. As quick as a flash he jumped to his feet, forgetting his full stomach and forgetting his basket of vegetables. The donkey had already headed off to a gateway in the corner of the courtyard and Chang Kuo Lau raced after him as quickly as his full stomach would allow. By now the teacher had come to his senses and was running across the courtyard, fists flailing, cursing the boy and his donkey.

Chang Kuo Lau took a running leap on to the donkey and landed facing the opposite direction to the donkey's head but there was no time to change his position. He just slapped the donkey's rump hard and off they went. At first Chang Kuo Lau was jolted as the donkey galloped across the stony earth outside the temple but gradually his ride became smoother. He looked down in amazement, the herb had given his donkey the power of flight and they sailed across the sky up to the heavens leaving the distraught teacher clutching the empty pan in despair.

According to legend, Chang Kuo Lau's abandoned reed chopsticks took root in the temple and grew into huge trees and to this day they are known far and wide as 'Kuo Lau trees'.

The Bamboo Shoot That Grows Upside Down

The townspeople knew very little about the woman who lived in a tumbledown cottage on the outskirts of Ch'ing Yuan town. Her husband had died shortly after the birth of her son and her only source of income came from the sale of large wickerwork baskets that she wove late into the night when her son was asleep. She always gave her son the most nourishing food and the best clothes she could afford. Each spring she picked tender young shoots from the bamboo grove behind her house which she used to make mouth watering stews for him. She survived on rice and watered broth made from the tough roots of the bamboo. Her clothes were old and patched and her health was weak. The townspeople knew she was a kindhearted and hardworking woman, but they rarely saw her. She dedicated her life to her only son and when he reached the age of eighteen she found him a suitable wife. She had, if anything, loved her son too much and failed to see that he had grown into a weak-willed man, afraid to argue with his wife and afraid to defend his mother.

All the household finances were arranged by her daughter-in-law, but the day-to-day chores were left to the old woman whose health was in decline after years of relentless hard work. Her sight was too weak to weave baskets, but each spring she was still forced to pick bamboo from the hill behind her house. Each time she raised her hands in protest she was verbally abused by her daughter-in-law while her son sat listlessly in the armchair. Each evening her son and daugher-in-law enjoyed stews made from the tender shoots and she was left to chew on the tough bamboo roots.

One evening as the family ate their dinner on the porch, Chang Kuo Lau, in the guise of an old beggar, came ambling from the direction of the bamboo forest towards their cottage. He stopped before them and bowed his head. He carefully noted the old woman sitting on a broken chair, trying hard to swallow the hard bamboo roots. He then turned his attention to the young couple obviously enjoying their evening meal and completely ignoring the old woman opposite them. He was amazed to see a mother treated with so little respect and raised a protest to the daughter-in-law. The young woman couldn't believe that a penniless beggar dared to criticise her. She grabbed her bowl of rice and threw it in the beggar's face, screaming, 'You lazy, good for nothing tramp. Mind your own business. Get out of my sight before I take my broom to you.'

But Chang Kuo Lau stood his ground. 'Do you think an old woman ought to be given bamboo roots to eat?' he demanded.

'What right do you have to criticise?' retorted the daughter-in-law. 'This old woman is used to eating bamboo roots. She's eaten them all her life. She enjoys them. My husband will confirm it.'

She elbowed her husband who had been shifting uncomfortably in his seat during this argument.

'Yes, yes, she's right,' he stuttered. 'My mother has always eaten bamboo roots as long as I can remember.'

Chang Kuo Lau was furious but he contained his anger. 'So you believe you are doing the right thing?' he said calmly.

'Yes, we do. We believe we are doing the best for her. We will never regret it,' they answered in unison.

'Even if you are struck down by thunder,' retorted Chang Kuo Lau.

'Even if we were killed by thunder, we'll never regret it,' answered the daughter-in-law defiantly.

'Well, I hope you eat bamboo shoots for ever,' said Chang Kuo Lau laughing, as he turned away from them.

He headed towards the bamboo grove behind their house and secretly pulled a bamboo shoot from one of the trees. He then quietly recited a spell over the shoot:

'Act obediently, bamboo,
Your point will be hard,
Your root will be soft,
The husband and wife will suffer,
The old woman will be happy.'

Chang Kuo Lau then plunged the bamboo shoot into the earth and left the grove.

From that time the bamboo shoots growing behind the house were rough and hard at their tip but tender and fleshy at the root. Chang Kuo Lau had not only put a spell on the bamboo grove, he had put a spell on the family so that the son and daughter-in-law were forced to eat the tips and the old woman always ate the soft roots.

To this day the bamboo shoots growing in Ch'ing Yuan are different to any other bamboo shoots throughout China. They are known as the 'Obedient Bamboo Shoots'.

How Chang Kuo Lau Obtained a Donkey

After their parents' death Chang Nan and his younger brother worked their small farm near the village of Chung Ts'iao Shan in Shansi province. They had always been happy in each other's company but all this changed when Chang Nan decided to marry. Chang Nan's wife found fault with everything her brother-in-law said or did and she eventually suceeded in turning the two brothers against each other. The quarrels became so bitter, it was impossible for all three to share the same house. Chang Kuo was forced to leave his home and take his meagre share of his inheritance – a well-worn quilt, one broken hoe, two wooden bowls and three earthenware dishes.

Chang Kuo made a new home in a disused hut on Yang Mei Hill, a day's donkey ride from his old home. He enjoyed the peace and solitude of his new home and spent most days picking wild fruits and mushrooms and growing sweet potatoes. Two months after settling in, Chang Kuo's sweet potatoes began to go missing. At first one or two were taken but eventually half the field was stolen.

One night Chang Kuo, carrying a heavy wooden stick, lay in wait for the thief. Shortly after midnight, an enormous black rabbit stealthily entered the field and began to nibble his sweet potatoes. Chang Kuo sprang out of his hiding place and charged towards the rabbit but he didn't move quickly enough. The rabbit had already bounded across the field and through a hole in the hedge. Chang Kuo pursued the rabbit as fast as his legs could carry him. The chase seemed to be endless. They pounded up and down three mountains, splashed across nine streams and trampled through thirty fields. Eventually the rabbit tried to make an escape into a large grotto but Chang Kuo saw him enter and fearlessly followed him in. When his eyes had become accustomed to the darkness, he looked around him. There was no doubt about it, someone had made this grotto their home. One room was furnished with a straw mattress covered with a colourful handwoven quilt, a round wooden table and two chairs. The second room was filled with wood, cooking oil, rice, chopsticks, pottery bowls, ploughing tools, a small stove and another straw mattress. Chang Kuo thought the owner was away until a voice behind him called his name.

'Chang Kuo, welcome to my house. Make yourself comfortable. I have prepared some hot tea and steamed buns for you.'

Chang Kuo swung around expecting to see a playful devil or ghost but all he saw was a big, black rabbit.

'Don't be startled,' reassured the rabbit. 'This is my home and I have brought you here to live with me.'

Chang Kuo hesitated for several moments and then rubbed his eyes to make sure he was not dreaming. No, the rabbit was real and he was talking to him but the last thing Chang Kuo would want to choose was a life with a thieving and talking rabbit. Chang Kuo gruffly declined the rabbit's suggestion. But the rabbit wouldn't take no for an answer.

'Please don't turn me down so carelessly,' begged the rabbit. 'I admit that I have been a thief. I have stolen everything you see in this grotto but that will change, I promise you. If you come to live with me, I will give up my life of crime and help you hunt in the forest. I know you are a poor man but I always knew that one day you would come here to live with me. That's why I led a life of petty crime. I did it for you.'

Chang Kuo mulled over the rabbit's words for several minutes and saw that the rabbit was right. He was a poor man and had nothing to lose. Chang Kuo replied gratefully, 'I trust you my friend and I will come and live with you.'

Chang Kuo moved into the grotto immediately, without a second thought for his old home or his humble belongings. That evening Chang Kuo received another unexpected surprise. As he was eating his evening meal, opposite the rabbit, a white mist slowly descended over the table and it became so thick Chang Kuo could barely see his chopsticks. Chang Kuo thought that nothing could surprise him after the shock earlier in the day but he was not prepared for the sight that greeted him when the mist cleared.

The black rabbit had changed into a fearsome, threatening black wolf. His smooth black ears were long and pointed. His sharp white teeth were bared and his black eyes glinted in the candlelight. Chang Kuo let his rice bowl and chopsticks fall to the floor but he was too stiff with fear to move from his seat. The wolf smiled, lifted its paw and laid it gently upon Chang Kuo's shaking hand. The wolf was his friend, not his enemy.

Chang Kuo nicknamed the wolf 'the Big Black One' and together they hunted in the forests and woods for miles around. The wolf was fearless and strong. It could cross thirty-three mountains in a day and ninety-nine streams at night. Foxes, stags, rabbits and even bears fell prey to the wolf's powerful jaws.

It was not long before Chang Kuo's brother and sister-in-law heard tales of their brother's hunting success and were soon consumed with jealousy. They spent hours plotting and scheming against the wolf and Chang Kuo and eventually decided to poison them by leaving steamed buns laced with arsenic outside the grotto door. But the wolf was not so easily fooled. He heard them approach, whispering conspiratorily, and then run away quickly. When they had gone the wolf emerged from the grotto, collected the buns in its claws, crept to Chang Nan's house and dropped the poisoned buns in the pigsty. The next morning, three of Chang Nan's pigs lay dead.

When Chang Nan and his wife discovered what had happened, they seized sharp kitchen knives and set out immediately for the wolf's grotto. They arrived at midnight and as they stealthily approached the grotto entrance the wolf pounced from the darkness, howling wildly and clawing ferociously. Chang Nan ran for his life but his wife was not so lucky, the wolf's teeth dug into her cotton jacket and trousers and ripped them from her back. Meanwhile Chang Kuo was woken up by the wolf's roar and ran from his bedroom believing the wolf had caught a wild bear. Instead he bumped into his embarrassed sister-in-law desperately trying to hide her nakedness. She pulled some fronds from a nearby tree, held them behind her and ran screaming into the woods.

After this second unsuccessful murder attempt, Chang Nan and is wife spent every waking hour plotting their revenge and eventually hit upon a solution. They visited the town judge and told him that Chang Kuo had purposefully and violently murdered their pigs. They demanded justice and at the same time handed him nine silver ounces as a bribe. The corrupt judge did not even try to discover the truth. He declared Chang Kuo guilty, summoned him to the court and punished him with forty lashes of a thonged leather whip. Chang Kuo stumbled from the courtroom and painfully returned to the grotto, so that the wolf could bathe his bloody wounds. But when he finally arrived at the grotto the wolf didn't run to greet him. In fact, the whole place had a silent eerie feel. He limped into the grotto and there, on the kitchen floor, lay the wolf's lacerated, limp body. In his absence the wolf had been murdered by Chang Nan and his wife.

Chang Kuo collapsed in tears at the sight of the wolf and over the next three days he rarely ate and only caught fitful snatches of sleep.

On the fourth evening, when he had fallen asleep from sheer exhaustion, the wolf spoke to him in a dream.

'Chang Kuo, don't cry. I have come to help you, so listen carefully to my words. In Hung Wen mountain there is a unicorn which can run a thousand miles a day and eight hundred miles a night. If you can catch this unicorn you will become immortal.'

Chang Kuo awoke from his dream with a start and ran swiftly from the grotto to Hung Wen mountain where he saw the unicorn grazing on the hill slopes. Its body was covered in golden scales and its curled horn was more than two feet in length. Chang Kuo crept cautiously towards the unicorn, but the alert creature heard his footsteps and bolted. Chang Kuo chased after it but the unicorn ran as fast as a

Chang Kuo Lau Chased the Unicorn (from a late 19th-century Chinese design)

meteor and jumped as quickly as lightning. Chang Kuo soon abandoned his chase and vowed never to waste his energy again until he could match the unicorn's speed.

Each day Chang Kuo dedicated fourteen hours to intensive running and jumping and within two months he had worn out nine thousand, nine hundred pairs of straw shoes. The skin on his feet was lined with three inches of hard and calloused skin and so he decided it was time to make a pair of iron shoes and went in search of a skilled blacksmith. After trudging the province he came across an old blacksmith's shop hidden from view in a street behind a temple. He entered the dimly lit workshop.

'Old master, could you make me a pair of iron shoes,' he asked respectfully.

The old blacksmith nodded his head and smiled knowingly. 'You are Chang Kuo, aren't you?' he asked even though he already knew Chang Kuo's story. 'The black wolf promised you immortality if you could catch the unicorn. That is why you want iron shoes. Am I right?'

'But how do you know this?' gasped Chang Kuo in surprise.

'I have telescopic eyes and catching wind ears. I can see and hear everything. If you acknowledge me as your master I will give you a priceless gift.'

Chang Kuo fell to his knees like a collapsing wall and called out 'Master' time and time again, until the old blacksmith put out his hands and raised Chang Kuo to his feet. The blacksmith then took a slip of paper in the shape of a donkey out of the black sleeve of his robe. He offered the donkey to Chang Kuo who drew back from the gift, convinced that the blacksmith was playing a trick on him.

'Master, a donkey runs slower than an ox, and a paper donkey can't even run an inch,' said Chang Kuo in disbelief.

The old blacksmith beckoned Chang Kuo to him, saying in hushed tones, 'I will tell you a secret. This donkey can run as fast as the unicorn. Watch me carefully.'

The old blacksmith placed the donkey on the floor and clapped his hands. The paper donkey rolled on the floor and up jumped a real donkey shaking its mane and pawing the ground in anticipation. Chang Kuo had never see such a graceful and powerful donkey. While he stood there admiring its strength the donkey gave a huge roar and galloped out of the workshop. Chang Kuo dashed after him and when he caught up with the donkey he took a great leap on to his back. Unfortunately the donkey changed direction at that very moment and Chang Kuo ended up clinging onto the donkey but

facing his tail instead of his head. He had no time to change his position, he simply grasped the donkey's thick coat of hair and held on
for dear life.

The donkey raced across the mountains and fields in search of the
unicorn. When they approached a wooded hillside they caught a
fleeting glimpse of the unicorn as he emerged from the forest under-
growth. The donkey and Chang Kuo followed in hot pursuit. When
the unicorn reached a sheer drop at the edge of a cliff it rose grace-
fully into the air. It was too late for Chang Kuo to stop the donkey as
he raced towards the precipitous cliff edge, so Chang Kuo shut his
eyes tightly, wrapped his arms around the donkey and prayed to the
gods. But the donkey didn't crash to the rocks below, he just flew
like the wind after the unicorn. They flew to the moon but just as
they caught up with the unicorn he landed in a fruit tree and
changed into a lunar fruit. The exhausted donkey and the disappointed Chang Kuo abandoned the chase at the foot of the fruit tree.
Chang Kuo collapsed against the tree trunk and buried his head in
his hands. He couldn't believe how close he had come to gaining
immortality. While he sat lamenting his bad fortune, a deep and
gentle voice called his name.

'Chang Kuo lift your head proudly. You will achieve immortality.'

Chang Kuo lifted his head in surprise. Before him stood the Jade
Emperor, resplendent in golden robes. The Jade Emperor raised his
arm and plucked a ripe lunar fruit from the tree and offered it to the
dumbfounded Chang Kuo who accepted it graciously. The minute
Chang Kuo bit into the fruit, his body was filled with surging energy
and he knew that he had gained immortality.

Chang Kuo rested on the moon for three days before returning to
earth on his donkey. But nothing had prepared him for the shock of
his return. His hair had turned white and decades had flown by in
his absence. Chang Kuo was now an old man. Everybody addressed
him as Chang Kuo Lau – Old Chang Kuo. And he still hadn't learnt to
ride his donkey properly. In fact he only knew one way to ride it,
and that was backwards.

Ts'ao Kuo Chiu
Repents His Sins

According to legend Ts'ao Kuao Chiu was one of five children born to Ts'ai Pin, a Chinese general of the Sung Dynasty. His only sister was declared queen when she was a young girl and so her four brothers were given royal status. But from the moment of their coronation, they abused this status by forming a powerful criminal gang. For many years they defrauded the government, operated a black market ring and organised large scale robberies and murders.

One day the gang heard about the imminent arrival of a wealthy jeweller to their city. He would be carrying a priceless pearl, the Resurrection pearl, the only one of its type in the world. They immediately mounted their horses and rode to the main road leading into the city. They found a secluded, tree-shaded spot in the road and waited in the shadows to ambush the jeweller and his retinue. Each brother carried a knife and a heavy wooden club, large enough to kill a man with one fierce blow. As the jeweller's carriage approached, the brothers jumped into the road brandishing their weapons before the terrified jeweller. The jeweller's horses bolted and his servants ran for their lives not even waiting to catch a glimpse of the armed robbers.

The brothers set upon the helpless jeweller, showering him with vicious blows and deep knife wounds. Within a few minutes they had collected their prize from the jeweller's cowskin purse hanging around his neck. They quickly buried his battered and bloody body in a shallow grave not far from the wood, but decided to leave the pearl on the jeweller's body and to return for it in the dead of night.

But fortune was against the brothers that day. No sooner had they galloped back to town, congratulating each other on such an efficient and successful attack, when a dog wandered into the trees where the jeweller's body lay buried. The dog sniffed the newly sealed earth, smelt blood and started to bark loudly. When noon came, it began to paw the shallow layer of earth and soon uncovered the jeweller's body. But on finding the body, the dog lost interest and ran away to chase rabbits in the wood, leaving the jeweller's mutilated corpse exposed to passersby.

Before long, two merchants came along discussing the tactics they would use to sell their silk cloth in the city. One merchant was arguing excitedly about his new plan for making money, when he stopped abruptly. His jaw dropped open and his face drained of colour. His friend turned to see what could have caused this transformation, and there, about twenty-five yards from where they stood, lay the dead jeweller. They did not even stop to examine the body but ran straight to Pao Kung, the wise magistrate in the city of Honar.

By dusk the magistrate and his guards had completely uncovered the unfortunate jeweller, but it was only when they searched his body that they discovered his priceless pearl and immediately recognised its power. They opened the jeweller's mouth and placed the Resurrection Pearl upon his tongue. Within a few moments the first tiny flicker of life appeared on the jeweller's eyelids. Before their eyes, the jeweller's gaping wounds began to heal, his bruises began to fade and his broken limbs were once again whole.

Within a day the jeweller was fully recovered. In fact, he felt healthier than he had for years. Pao Kung suspected the brothers' involvement in the murder and the jeweller was able to confirm his suspicions. The brothers were bound in chains and brought before the magistrate for trial. Because the jeweller had been brought back to life, the gang could not be sentenced to death for the crime of murder but the death penalty hung over them if they committed any other crime, even the most minor one.

This frightening episode brought Ts'ao Kuo Chiu to his senses, but it only convinced the other brothers of their good fortune in their life of crime. Ts'ao Kuo Chiu could no longer keep company with them since they had lost his trust and respect. Not long after his lucky escape from the death sentence, Ts'ao Kuo Chiu became a hermit, dedicating his life to the study of Taoism, but his brothers' zeal for crime was untouched. They were caught defrauding the treasury and, as they had been warned by Pao Kung, they were publically beheaded. But Ts'ao Kuo Chiu knew nothing of their fate. He had drawn apart from this world and after thirty years of Taoist study he was raised to the sky to join the Immortals.

How Ho Hsien Ku
Became an Immortal

An old woman owned a small farm at the foot of Mi-Lo Shan. She had never completed a full day's work and had no intention of doing so. As the years progressed she had become lazier and lazier, spending most of the day maliciously gossiping with her neighbours or giving abrupt orders to her servant.

Her latest servant was a young, beautiful and generous hearted girl called Ho Hsien Ku. However hard she worked the old woman was never satisfied. She continually harangued, scolded and punished the helpless girl. Ho Hsien Ku's day began at five o'clock in the morning and rarely finished before midnight.

Besides clearing the house and preparing the food she had to plant and reap the crops and feed and care for the animals. Ho Hsien Ku did this without complaint in return for food and lodgings, but at night, when she fell exhausted on to her straw mattress, she silently wept herself to sleep.

One day the old woman set off to visit her cousin, leaving the young girl to guard the house. Ho Hsien Ku placed a small wicker chair outside the front door and sat down with her sewing basket to repair the old woman's clothes.

Through the haze of the hot afternoon sun, she saw seven figures moving slowly towards her. As they drew closer, she saw their ragged clothes, gaunt faces and downcast eyes. The beggars eventually gathered around her. One stepped forward and in pleading tones addressed Ho Hsien Ku. 'Could you please help us. We have not eaten a morsel of food in five days and now we are starving. Could you spare us a bowl of rice.'

Ho Hsien Ku was moved by their distress. If she had had the choice, she would have given the beggars all the food in the house but she was hesitant. The old woman meticulously checked the amount of food in the house each day. If a handful of rice or a spoonful of oil was missing, she would beat the girl mercilessly. But Ho Hsien Ku could not turn the beggars away. She would rather be beaten black and blue than let these unfortunate ragged men starve by the roadside.

She beckoned the beggars to rest on the straw mats in front of the house then went into the kitchen to boil a pan of rice. Ten minutes later each beggar had a bowl of rice in his hands which he devoured eagerly and gratefully. The rice gave them renewed strength and after thanking Ho Hsien Ku profusely, the beggars wandered in the direction of the nearest town. No sooner had they disappeared from view, when the old woman returned home. Without acknowledging Ho Hsien Ku, she marched straight into the kitchen to check the rice, noodles, eggs, fish, oil and wood. Ho Hsien Ku sat trembling outside the door and within a few minutes a piercing scream of anger came from the kitchen. The old woman ran from the kitchen brandishing a wooden broom.

'You thief, you ungrateful wretch! What have you done with my rice? Have you eaten it or sold it?' she demanded as she held the girl's arm with a vice-like grip.

Holding back her tears, Ho Hsien Ku recounted the whole story but the old woman had a heart like iron. 'I have no pity for these dirty beggars. You either find them and bring them back to me or I will beat your legs till you can no longer walk.'

The old woman loosened her grip on Ho Hsien Ku's arm, just enough for Ho Hsien Ku to break free and dash after the beggars. She eventually caught up with them as they were resting by the dusty roadside. Standing breathlessly before them she pleaded desperately.

'I am sorry to ask you this, but could you return with me to prove to my mistress that you ate the rice. If you do not come she will beat me black and blue.'

The beggars were only too willing to help the girl who had taken pity on them and they returned home with her. The old woman was still in a furious temper when they arrived.

'How dare you eat the food that belongs to a poor old woman,' she screamed. 'I demand that you vomit every morsel on the floor in front of me. If you don't, I will make sure that nobody in this district offers you food or water. You deserve to starve.'

The beggars had no choice but to do as they were told. One by one they vomited the noodles on to the packed earth floor in front of the house. The old woman then turned to Ho Hsien Ku and demanded vehemently, 'Eat every single noodle that has been vomited. This is the price you have to pay for feeding dirty beggars.'

She pushed the tearful and frightened Ho Hsien Ku to the floor and the helpless girl was forced to put a handful of the vomited noodles into her mouth. As soon as the noodles touched her tongue she felt her body become lighter and lighter. She felt her legs rise from the ground and her body began to float away from the spiteful old woman, away from the home where she had suffered so miserably.

The old woman began to panic and turned round to demand an explanation from the beggars, but they too had risen high above the house. She caught a last glimpse of the beggars before they disappeared into the clouds and her servant, Ho Hsien Ku, was in their midst.

The Seven Immortals had come to earth to test the young girl's character and she had proved herself worth of immortality. Because she had endured suffering without complaint and given to the poor without thought for herself, she could work alongside the Immortals for eternity.

A Hundred Birds in a Mountain

The Eight Immortals had spent days resting on Huang Shan mountain but when it was time to return home Ho Hsien Ku could not bear the thought of leaving. She was so struck by the mountain's tranquil beauty that she decided to spend some time there alone.

She usually rose at dawn to pray and meditate and spent the rest of the day on the mountain's slopes. One morning, as she carefully made her way along a narrow path she came across an old man whistling cheerfully as he carried a bamboo pole on his shoulder. The long pole was crowded with birds of all colours and shapes. Some sang, some hopped along the pole and others flew into the air only to return again to the pole. At first, Ho Hsien Ku was startled to meet someone on this usually deserted path, but then she was inquisitive.

'I have travelled every inch of China, but I have never seen birds as tame or beautiful as your birds,' she complimented him, at the same time expecting an explanation.

But the old man remained silent. He glanced at the straw basket under her arm which was overflowing with fragrant and unusual flowers and grasses. He felt like telling her that he had never seen such a basket of colourful flowers before but he held his tongue. For a long while, Ho Hsien Ku and the old man stared at each other. Ho Hsien Ku grew uncomfortable with this silence. Although he had human eyes and a human body, he had an unusual presence and why did he keep glancing at her basket of flowers? How could he possibly know that she was an Immortal and that her basket of flowers had no bottom and no edges, that it could contain all the flowers in the world and still have room for more.

She decided to test him and asked him scornfully, 'I suppose you have a hundred different species of bird on your pole and you know the name of each one, and I suppose there are a hundred differrent species of bird on this mountain and you know where to find them?'

The old man was completely unmoved by her question and simply replied, 'I suppose your flower basket can produce more than a thousand varieties of flowers and grasses?'

'Tell me the truth,' demanded Ho Hsien Ku. 'You are not human.

No human could ever guess the secret of my basket. Now tell me what you want and what you are doing here.'

The old man once more fell silent. He knew only too well the identity of the woman before him. He knew how she had achieved immortality and he knew that she was sometimes too confident and too glib with this precious gift. Now was the time to teach her a lesson.

'I am afraid that your flower basket is not complete. It does not contain any flowers or grasses from this mountain,' he said with authority.

Ho Hsien Ku could feel anger rising from deep within her. She had been immortal for more than a hundred years and no one had ever dared to challenge her authority.

'What do you mean?' she demanded. 'I have scoured every field and mountain in every direction that the wind blows. I have picked flowers that no human has ever set eyes upon and you have the audacity to tell me that I haven't found something growing on Huang Shan mountain.'

'That's exactly what I am telling you,' retorted the old man, as he picked up a bundle of grass from the soft earth nearby. He held the grass out to her. 'You do not have this fragrant grass in your basket.'

Ho Hsien Ku reached out for the grass. She felt its texture, she examined its colour, and she smelt the delicate aroma. But she was too proud to admit defeat.

'This is nothing but a bunch of wild weeds, the sort of weeds that can be found on any hill slope and in any field throughout China. Do you take me for a fool? I can distinguish weeds from aromatic grass. The plants in my basket will prove that to you.'

The old man stared at her but said nothing in reply.

'Stop showing off,' she demanded petulantly. 'You have indicated that Huang Shan has one hundred different types of birds. Well, where are they?'

'That's easy to answer,' replied the old man calmly. 'Follow me up the mountain and I will show you.'

The old man climbed steadily up the steep mountain tracks and Ho Hsien Ku followed reluctantly in his footsteps. As they rounded a steep spur of the mountain they were greeted with a view of the full majesty of the 'Lotus Peak'.

'Now is the time to test him,' though Ho Hsien Ku. 'I want to see a peacock,' she demanded haughtily.

'I will show you a peacock,' answered the old man and he pointed to the 'Lotus Peak'.

Ho Hsien Ku followed his gaze and he had been right. The craggy rocks of the 'Lotus Peak' were shaped like the fully opened wings of a peacock trying to make an ascent. But Ho Hsien Ku was not completely satisfied and demanded to see a swan. The old man pointed at a pavillion carved from the pale grey rock of the mountain. And there, at the top of the pavillion was a rock with the perfect contours of a swan, its slender neck raised to the heavens. Underneath the swan's feet, lay many small stones, each with the smooth oval-shaped form of an egg.

Having seen this, Ho Hsien Ku felt her confidence slipping away and could not summon up the courage to ask any more questions. She gazed around her in defeat and despair and suddenly it dawned on her that every rock and stone had the contours of a bird. The 'Nine Dragon Peak' was in the shape of an owl, the 'White Hill' in the distance looked like a flock of magpies and even the stones by her feet looked like swallows. The old man knew that she had learnt her lesson and to save her any more embarrassment he drew her attention to the birds of his bamboo pole.

'Look at this bird. It is a rare Shan T'ung bird. Here is a silver pheasant and over here are two "falling in love birds".'

Ho Hsien Ku watched two small birds with red beaks and multicoloured feathers coo gently over one another. The old man was willing to describe the ninety-six other birds on the bamboo pole, but Ho Hsien Ku's face was as red as a crab in boiling water and he knew that he had proved his point.

Ho Hsien Ku bowed her head before the old man and asked respectfully, 'Why is the grass on this mountain different from the grass already in my basket?'

The old man took her hand gently. 'Look at me,' he said. 'My face is unwrinkled and I have no beard but my hair is white. Think carefully, I think you know me.'

Ho Hsien Ku gave a gasp of recognition. It was Hsien Yoah Huang Ti, the Yellow Emperor, skilled in alchemy and knowledgeable in immortality-giving drugs. When he rose to the heavens to be with the gods, many people wanted to follow him to achieve immortality. They grabbed hold of his beard but their weight ripped the hairs from his chin and they fell back to earth. His hairs were carried by the wind to Huang Shan mountain and took root in the fertile soil. The aromatic grass was 'Dragon Beard' grass.

Ho Hsien Ku knelt down before the old man to beg his forgiveness.

'I have been foolish and proud, my wise brother and I now kneel before you to beg your pardon,' she said humbly.

The Yellow Emperor bent down and took her hand.

'Get up my immortal sister,' he said kindly. 'You must remember that every person, animal and plant is important no matter how small it is. Do not be critical of the world around you. Take your basket and throw your flowers to the wind and in return I will tell the birds on my bamboo pole to fly away and nest in every bush and tree on this mountain.'

Ho Hsien Ku did as she was commanded and that is why to this day Huang Shan mountain is vibrant with birdsong and colourfully decked with flowers.

The Prophecies of
Han Hsiang Tzu

When Han Hsiang Tzu was a young child, he was sent to live with his uncle, Han Yu, a great scholar and poet. He loved to study the ancient philosophies and try to divine the secrets of the Immortals. Han Yu soon realised that his little nephew was no ordinary scholar. Within a short period of time, Han Hsiang Tzu was writing better poetry and essays than his uncle. His uncle, a kindly man, was delighted.

One day, Han Hsiang Tzu took a little pot filled with earth. He passed his hand over it and a beautiful flowering plant arose from the soil. On the leaves were written some verses:

The clouds cover Ch'in Ling Shan.
Where now do you live?
The snow lies thick upon Lan Kuan.
Your horse will go no further.

Han Yu asked 'What is the meaning of this poem?' But his nephew would only say that his uncle would soon know.

Not long after, Han Yu was involved in something which upset the Emperor. He was sent in disgrace to the south. When he reached Lan Kuan, the snow was indeed too thick for his horse to pass through. Suddenly, Han Hsiang Tzu appeared and swept the snow aside. Han Yu knew then that his nephew was destined to become an immortal.

The time came for Han Hsiang Tzu to leave his uncle's house and instruction and the two friends gave each other a poem. Han Yu gave his nephew the following:

Most of those who live on earth seek only for the heady pleasures of honour and wealth.
You alone, have continued faithfully to follow the true Tao.
The time will come when you will rise into the sky.
Travelling to Heaven, you will show others the true Tao.

In this way, Han Yu predicted that Han Hsiang Tzu would become an immortal. But Han Hsiang Tzu's prophecy was not so optimistic for Han Yu:

There have been many great men who have served our country,
But none of them can be compared to you in understanding of
literature.
When you have achieved a high official position,
You will end by being buried in a rainy and foggy country.

Han Yu was very disturbed by this and Han Hsiang Tzu was
moved by his distress. There was nothing he could do to stop the
events happening, so instead he gave his uncle a magic potion
which would bring him back to life and thereby enable him to return
to his own country and family.

All that Han Hsiang Tzu had prophecied came true, but using the
magic potion, Han Yu was able to return from the dead and was re-
stored to the arms of his loving family.

The Dragon Girl and
the Immortal Flute

Han Hsiang Tzu was excellent company. He was a talented flute player who inspired others with his vivacious love of life. At one moment his music could express happiness and exhilaration and at the next, sadness and heartbreak.

He played from dawn to sunset never tiring of his flute's sweet notes. Wherever he travelled he attracted a cheerful audience who accompanied him with lively singing and dancing.

One autumn his wanderings led him to the shores of the Eastern Sea, home of the beautiful and musically gifted dragon girls. As the last rays of the sun slanted across the calm sea he began to play a soft, lilting tune which was carried across the sea by a gentle evening breeze.

It reached the ears of the dragon girls who had been singing to each other far away from the shore. Their voices fell silent as they caught snatches of this heavenly music and although they were tempted to see who could play the flute so sweetly, they were too embarrassed to approach the shore. That is all except one, the most beautiful and the most talented, the seventh daughter of the Dragon King. She was consumed with a desire to catch a glimpse of Han Hsiang Tzu but it was imperative that she kept her identity secret and so she changed into an eel. She swam close to the shore where she could swim unseen beneath the surface of the water, but she forgot that the tide was slowly drawing out and within the hour her smooth silver body was in full view of Han Hsiang Tzu. But the princess was so enraptured with the music she failed to notice the retreating tide. She slithered and rolled, rocked and swayed under Han Hsiang Tzu's enchanted glance. He had never seen such an unusual eel, an eel who seemed to understand his music and appreciate it.

'My precious eel,' he cried out. 'I have heard of the beauty of the seventh dragon princess. Send her my humble regards.'

Han Hsiang Tzu sighed hopelessly. 'If only the eel could understand my words, but that is too much to hope for,' he thought to himself. But the eel did seem to respond. It slithered closer, gazing attentively, and once more began its graceful dance. Han Hsiang

Tzu took the flute to his mouth and began to play a mournful tune. The eel slipped closer and closer and before Han Hsiang Tzu's astonished gaze it began to change form.

Through the shadowy twilight, he saw the eel become larger and larger, as its silver skin fell away to reveal pale flawless skin. The radiant face of a woman appeared. Her thick black hair fell to her waist, her radiant face shone with pleasure and her body swayed to the music. Han Hsiang Tzu was afraid she might go as quickly as she had come and so he didn't dare take his flute from his lips. He played as he had never played before, the feelings in his heart pouring out through his music. She danced and she danced, her gaze transfixed on his silhouette. Han Hsiang Tzu closed his eyes for a brief moment but when he opened them she had gone, disappeared beneath the waves.

He played late into the night but no song, however sweet, could make her return. At dawn, he fell exhausted on the sand. He woke at midday and without a thought for food or water he began to play again. As the sun began to set, his efforts were rewarded. The eel appeared as it had done the night before and the events of the previous night were repeated. The same thing happened the following night, but all this time the princess did not utter a single word.

By now Han Hsiang Tzu could think of nothing else but the stunning princess, but on the fourth night she failed to appear as usual. He played every love song he could remember and called to her across the dark night but his efforts were in vain. In despair he threw his flute on to the jagged rocks where it splintered into hundreds of fragments. Han Hsiang Tzu fell to his knees and wept. He was so wrapped up in his world of sorrow that he failed to hear an old woman cross the shore and crouch beside him. He jumped up in surprise when she gently tapped him on the shoulder.

'I'm sorry to frighten you,' she said, 'but I saw you weeping and came over to offer you my help. Listen to what I have to say but do not ask me any questions. The princess cannot come. Her father has discovered her secret and chained her deep within the Sea Palace. He has forbidden her to ever see you again. But I have one consolation for you. The princess asked to give you this piece of immortal bamboo.'

Han Hsiang Tzu accepted the long, brown, bamboo stick gratefully. He fashioned a flute from this gift, a flute that could compose mesmerising music that never failed to enchant those who heard it. But Han Hsiang Tzu had lost interest in human company and instead chose to live a solitary life in the caves and grottoes of remote mountains.

When Han Hsiang Tzu finally attained immortality, he still took his flute with him on all his travels. The music had the power to destroy evil spirits and defeat demons but it did not have the power to bring back the dragon princess. She had stolen the immortal bamboo from Kuan Yin's forest and the theft did not go unnoticed. As a punishment she was forced to become Kuan Yin's maid-in-waiting for eternity.

Even today the fishermen of the Eastern Sea claim that they can hear the soft notes of a flute carried by the wind. It is Han Hsiang Tzu calling the dragon princess to him, but she can never return.

The Flower Basket Epiphany

Lan Ts'ai Ho loved to travel the length and breadth of China collecting flowers, plants and grasses. He knew the name of every plant whether they grew on the lowland marshes or on mountain peaks, so when he heard about rare black chrysanthemums and stone lilies growing on Hua Shan mountain he had to see them with his own eyes.

Lan Ts'ai Ho arrived at Hua Shan on a clear, sunny day. The slopes were blanketed with spring flowers and the air was filled with bees and butterflies, but no matter how hard he searched he couldn't find a black chrysanthemum or a stone lily. Exhausted from his walk he leaned against a smooth, sun-warmed rock to take a well earned rest. As soon as he had settled himself he saw two rabbits, with red flowers in their mouths, scuttling towards a nearby cave. Unable to contain his curiousity he cautiously followed the rabbits inside the cave. Instead of entering a damp, mossy shelter he was greeted with the sight of a verdant garden teeming with flowers and to his delight he saw an abundance of black chrysanthemums and stone lilies in full flower.

Lan Ts'ai Ho was not only amazed to find rare flowers but also to see the flowers of the four seasons growing at the same time and in the same place. He sat down against the cave wall intoxicated by the beauty and fragrance around him and there he stayed until daybreak. As the first rays of sunlight filtered through the cave entrance, Lan Ts'ai Ho was awoken from his trance by a rustling sound coming from the darkest corner of the cave. He stood up, careful not to damage the flower bed, and slowly made his way to the back of the cave. Peering through the gloom he made out the shape of a finely woven flower basket resting on a stone slab. The rustling noise was definitely coming from the basket, but before Lan Ts'ai Ho could get close enough to see what was in the basket there was a bright flash of light and a wizened old woman appeared out of the basket.

Lan Ts'ai Ho was rooted to the spot, speechless with surprise, but the old woman spoke gently and reassuringly to him.

'Don't be afraid, my friend. I can see that you take great pleasure from my flowers. I have cultivated these flowers all my life. If I could,

I would change this world into a garden overflowing with flowers. My basket is a precious gift from the gods and on command it can produce enough flowers to fill a valley. I want you to borrow it and use it wisely.'

She laid the basket carefully at Lan Ts'ai Ho's feet and then disappeared as quickly as she had appeared.

Lan Ts'ai Ho gingerly lifted the basket on to his arm and threaded his way through the flower beds and out into the cool morning air. By mid-morning he had arrived at the nearest village. The local traders were busy selling their wares on both sides of the main street and in the dark, narrow side lanes he caught glimpses of children playing, women hanging out their washing and small groups of men drinking tea and talking intently.

He stopped for a moment to buy a mango from a street trader and his attention was drawn by the sound of a bitter quarrel and a woman crying. Thinking he might be of use, Lan Ts'ai Ho turned into a nearby lane to see what was happening. Three men and one woman stood outside a small burnt-out flower shop. All of them seemed to be gesticulating and crying at once. As far as Lan Ts'ai Ho could gather, Wei the flower seller had refused to let his daughter, Wei Mei-Chen, become the unwilling concubine of a wealthy landowner.

He had already given permission for his daughter to marry a poor but trustworthy student named Fan. The landowner, Sai Ch'ien Sui, had not taken kindly to Wei's decision and in the dead of night he had sent a gang of thugs to burn down Wei's flower shop. By the time Lan Ts'ai Ho arrived Fan lay unconscious on the floor and Sai Ch'ien Sui was threatening Wei's life if he could not have Wei's daughter as a concubine. Before Lan Ts'ai Ho could do anything the wealthy landowner and the tearful woman had disappeared into the maze of lanes and alleyways in the village.

Lan Ts'ai Ho approached the old man to comfort him but the old man was beyond comfort. 'You don't understand the situation,' Wei stammered through his tears. 'She is gone forever. The moment she enters Sai's family she will never return.'

Lan Ts'ai Ho listened respectfully then bent down and pulled a handful of seeds from the flower basket and threw them on the floor. Within a few seconds green shoots sprouted from the dry earth and a few seconds later they burst into vivid flowers. Lan Ts'ai Ho plucked two of these flowers and held them under Fan's nose. Soon the unconscious student began to stir and mumble. Then, before Wei's unbelieving eyes, Fan sneezed twice, woke up and rose to his feet, feeling fit and healthy. This was enough to persuade Wei that Lan Ts'ai Ho, above all others, might be able to rescue his daughter.

Wei led Lan Ts'ai Ho to Sai Ch'ien Sui's house, but left him at the gates for fear of being beaten or tortured. Lan Ts'ai Ho confidently called to the guards who approached him, but, realising that he was of little importance, promptly ignored him. But as luck would have it, an old steward was approaching the gates with a parcel for Sai Ch'ien Sui. Lan Ts'ai Ho beckoned to him. 'Good steward, could you please tell your master that Lan Ts'ai Ho the flower seller is here to see him.'

'But how can you be a flower seller when there are no flowers in your basket?' asked the steward with suspicion.

Lan Ts'ai Ho drew out two seeds, put one in the steward's right palm and the other in his left palm. He then picked up some soil and let it trickle on to the steward's palms. Within ten seconds a fragrant peony had flowered in the steward's left palm and an aromatic chrysanthemum had flowered in the steward's right palm. While the steward stood dumbfounded by Lan Ts'ai Ho's magic, Sai Ch'ien Sui's angry voice could be heard from within the house. He was in the middle of scolding Wei Mei-Chen for her disobedience, but he stopped in mid-sentence when the aroma of the magic flowers wafted in through the window. He ran to the door where he saw the steward with two flowers growing in his palms. Sai Ch'ien Sui reached out to pick the flowers, but as he touched them they turned into mandarin ducks which immediately flew out of his grasp.

'Where did you learn this wonderful trick,' Sai Ch'ien Sui asked the steward in astonishment, leading him into the room.

'It is not my trick, master,' replied the steward. 'The flower seller, who is waiting to see you at the gate, put two seeds in my hands and they miraculously turned into flowers.'

'Bring him to me immediately,' demanded Sai Ch'ien Sui. 'I want him to dine on my finest meat and my most expensive wines.'

But before the steward had a chance to say anything, Lan Ts'ai Ho came swaggering into the room dressed in silk and satin robes. Sai Ch'ien Sui was duly impressed and sat this talented magician in a place of honour. The dinner table was soon laid, but before Lan Ts'ai Ho put a morsel of food to his lips, his eager host offered him ten ounces of silver to perform his magic. Lan Ts'ai Ho politely declined this payment. It was enough to accept his host's hospitality and in return he would perform his magic. Lan Ts'ai Ho placed his flower basket at Sai Ch'ien Sui's feet. Then he placed two seeds at the bottom of the basket, poured a bowl of wine on to the seeds, and, before his host could blink, the basket changed into a verdant garden teaming with flowers and birds.

Although Sai Ch'ien Sui was impressed by this magic he looked perplexed and worried. He turned to Lan Ts'ai Ho and spoke hesitantly, 'I realise that this is not human magic and your presence gives me a strange sensation. Are you one of the Eight Immortals?'

Lan Ts'ai Ho nodded but remained silent. Sai Ch'ien Sui heaved a sigh of satisfaction and continued more confidently. 'I have one great wish and perhaps you can make this come true. I am desperate to win the love of a beautiful girl called Wei Mei-Chen, but each time I approach her she spurns me. Can you help me win her love?'

Lan Ts'ai Ho gave a knowing smile before offering Sai Ch'ien Sui some reassuring advice.

'Why pick on one girl when there are so many attractive women in this word? You could have your choice of the world's most beautiful women.'

Saying this, he plucked a peony, crumpled it in his hand and threw the crushed petals high into the air. As the petals came floating down, they changed into seven stunning young girls singing and dancing in perfect harmony.

Sai Ch'ien Sui had never seen such beauty before and his eyes followed every move of their graceful limbs. He was particularly taken by the curvaceous body and dark eyes of a girl in a finely woven green silk dress. Lan Ts'ai Ho saw a lascivious leer spread across Sai Ch'ien Sui's face and so, with a clap of his hands, he made the girls disappear into thin air.

'Bring them back, bring them back,' begged Sai Ch'ien Sui, jumping to his feet. Lan Ts'ai Ho refused to recall them but he did promise other remarkable tricks to satisfy his host.

The two men passed an enjoyable week together, eating and drinking to their hearts' content. Each evening after dinner, Lan Ts'ai Ho would perform an original trick and on the seventh evening Sai Ch'ien Sui asked for a special request.

'My talented friend, could you please conjure up the girl in the green silk dress. I haven't been able to take my thoughts off her for this past week.'

Lan Ts'ai Ho could not refuse such a request from his generous host. He promised to make the girl appear but on one condition. She must be exchanged for Wei Mei-Chen.

'Of course you can have Wei Mei-Chen,' replied Sai Ch'ien Sui eagerly. 'I thought you had your eye on her. Accept her as a gift, I'm bored of her reticence.'

Lan Ts'ai Ho nodded his head in thanks and politely withdrew from the dinner table on the pretence of collecting an important parcel from the nearby village. He picked up his flower basket and quickly left, leaving his host smiling contentedly in anticipation of the delights to come. Lan Ts'ai Ho arrived breathless and excited at Wei's house.

'Your worries are over,' he assured Wei, who had hardly slept since his daughter's abduction.

'You are coming with me to collect your daughter,' continued Lan Ts'ai Ho. 'You and Fan must jump into my flower basket immediately. We don't want to waste any time.'

'Now hold on, my good friend,' replied Wei. 'Have you been drinking too much tonight? How can two fully grown men fit into a flower basket?'

'Stop wasting time,' cried Lan Ts'ai Ho. 'Do you want to see your daughter again or don't you? If you want proof, I'll jump into the flower basket myself but we're only wasting time while we argue about this. Just trust me.'

Wei and Fan had no choice. They gingerly approached the flower basket, stepped into it and promptly disappeared from view.

After checking they were comfortable, Lan Ts'ai Ho pulled the basket into the crook of his arm and returned hastily to Sai Ch'ien Sui's house. Wei Mei-Chen was already waiting in the reception room. Her face was stained with tears and her clothes were dishevelled and torn. Lan Ts'ai Ho spoke gently to her. 'Your father and husband-to-be are waiting here for you.'

So saying, he waved his hand at the flower basket and out jumped Wei and Fan. They held the frightened girl in their arms until her tears subsided.

'Go quickly,' ordered Lan Ts'ai Ho. 'If Sai Ch'ien Sui discovers the truth he will murder all of you.'

The reunited family fled the house without looking back. Sai Ch'ien Sui had heard the commotion in the reception room and soon emerged to discover Lan Ts'ai Ho standing alone.

'Where's the girl you promised me? I want to see her now. Make her appear.'

Lan Ts'ai Ho fulfilled his promise and with another wave of his hand she appeared before them. Flowers were interwined through her long black hair, her eyes were downcast and her perfect figure was silhouetted against the light of the doorway.

She took one small step towards Lan Ts'ai Ho. 'What can I do for you, sir?' she asked gently and quietly.

'You are to stay with Sai Ch'ien Sui and do whatever he asks,' replied Lan Ts'ai Ho.

She nodded her head in acceptance. Meanwhile Sai Ch'ien Sui walked around and around the girl, his eyes wide with delight. He eventually took her by the hand and led her into his private sitting room. A minute later screams of anger reverberated throughout the house. Sai Ch'ien Sui's voice rose hysterically.

'You devil, you liar, you have cheated me. You have deceived me with your vile magic.'

The anxious steward flung open the doors of the sitting room where he expected to see the young girl in the arms of his master, but instead he saw his master lying motionless on the tiled floor. Where the girl had once been, he clutched a torn and ragged bamboo pillow.

P'eng Cho and the
Eight Immortals

Once, in a distant and remote part of China, there lived a simple peasant boy, P'eng Cho. His father had died when he was very young, and his mother had never remarried. She respected her husband too much for that. P'eng Cho and his mother lived together outside a little village. Life was tough and the pair of them had barely enough to eat. But P'eng Cho was a good and dutiful son and his mother took great delight in him. Every day, P'eng Cho would take the ox out to plough the fields and to earn enough for them both to live.

One day, as he was ploughing a field, a fortune teller passed by. Impressed by the hard working young boy, the fortune teller stopped and looked at him. A look of concern came over his face and he beckoned the young boy to him.

'I have looked at the five features of your face and read your fortune. I must warn you that you will die on your twentieth birthday,' said the fortuune teller as he shook his head in sadness and then continued on his way. P'eng Cho was deeply upset, but continued with his work until nightfall.

That evening, P'eng Cho told his mother what the fortune teller had said. She was distraught with grief, but she was helpless. The wise man must have given an accurate prediction.

Not many years later, the Eight Immortals were walking past P'eng Cho's paddy fields and decided to cut across the narrow causeway which divided the watery expanses. When P'eng Cho saw the distinguished company coming his way, he pulled the ox to one side and held him still to avoid splashing them. The Eight Immortals were impressed with the thoughtfulness of the young man and commented to each other on his nobility of spirit.

That night, when he returned home, P'eng Cho told his mother about the eight strangers. His mother immediately knew that they must be the Eight Immortals. She urged her son that if they passed by again, he was to ask for their help.

Time passed. At long last P'eng Cho's twentieth birthday arrived. His mother was beside herself with grief and sent him out to work, not knowing if she would ever see him again. P'eng Cho ploughed his field, his heart filled with sadness. Suddenly, he saw the Eight Immortals coming across the fields. He ran and fell on his knees before them, begging them to save him from his fate. The Eight Immortals, who knew well what lay in store, asked him to explain. P'eng Cho told them about the fortune teller's prediction. 'If you can possibly help me, please do so,' he cried.

The Eight Immortals recalled what a noble spirit this young man had. They also knew of his poor mother and of how well he cared for her. So they agreed to grant him an extra one hundred years of life. The young man leapt up with joy and surprise, and as he did so, he dropped his hoe.

P'eng Cho did indeed live another one hundred years. But he had failed to realise that when his hoe had fallen, it had killed a small but deadly snake. It was this snake which would have ended his life, had it not been for the Eight Immortals.

Han Tzu and the Young Master

There was once a simple, kind man by the name of Han Tzu. He had never read a book in his life, but he seemed to know the ways of animals and of nature better than the wisest sage. This was why he was called Han Tzu – Tzu means wise Master.

For many years Han Tzu had served his master well. The old man respected his loyal and wise servant and treated him like one of the family. At all the great festivals, Han Tzu stood with the family. When there was joy in the family, Han Tzu celebrated. When there was sadness, Han Tzu mourned or wept. For him, his master's family was his own and he lived a happy and contented life, watching the movement of the stars, the ways of the animals and patterns of nature as he went about his daily business.

Han Tzu worked with his master, who was a goldsmith. Han Tzu was a fine craftsman and made the most beautiful pieces of jewellery. Then one day, the old master died. The funeral procession was the largest ever seen and many came to offer their condolences, but no one was more heartbroken than Han Tzu.

At the death of the goldsmith, the new master of the house returned from a faraway province. Han Tzu had watched the new master grow up as a child and had often saved little creatures from the cruel hands of the boy and set them free. The new master was a hard and vicious man who hated the memory of his father. Within days, life became unbearable in the house and Han Tzu did not know what to do. He felt as though his whole life had collapsed about him. All he wanted was to work in the goldsmith shop, study the ways of nature and do no harm to anyone. Yet it did not seem as if this simple request would be fulfilled. What was he to do?

Meanwhile, the young master hated the simple man who had crossed him as a child. One day, while a group of other young men, friends of his, were in the shop he turned to Han Tzu and said, 'You thief, I saw you. You just stole some gold. You may have been able to fool my father, but you cannot fool me. I know you have been stealing from us from the very first day you came to this house. Let's grab him and show him how we punish thieves.'

Before Han Tzu could speak or move a muscle, the young men

jumped upon him and beat him up. They tied his hands roughly and dragged him out of the house. With loud shouts, they pushed and pulled him through the streets saying that they had caught a thief and were now going to punish him.

It happened that the Eight Immortals were passing through the city that day. Hearing the noise, they asked someone what was going on.

'They say they have caught a thief red-handed and will now punish him. But it's old Han Tzu whom they have caught. He never did anyone any harm.'

The Eight Immortals looked at each other and without saying a word they followed the excited crowd. When they reached the place of public execution, the young men stopped and prepared to hang poor Han Tzu. At that moment, Lu Tung Pin stepped forward wearing the clothes of a high official. 'What is going on here? What evidence do you have to hang this man?'

The young men stopped, afraid that this might be an official of the Emperor.

'We found this gold upon him,' said the new master. 'He stole it from us.'

Lu Tung Pin winked at Ti Kuai Li. 'You,' he said, pointing at Lan Ts'ai Ho as though he had never seen him before, 'bring me this gold, for it is growing dark and no one can see it properly.'

So Lan Ts'ai Ho stepped forward and took the gold. In an instant he closed his hand over it and the gold turned to yellow lumps of clay. Lu Tung Pin looked at the clay. 'Gold, you say!' he exclaimed. 'What kind of gold do you have in this city? You are lying. You have even tried to frame an innocent man. I should have you executed for false accusations.'

The young men turned and stared at the new master. 'It was his fault sir,' they cried. The young master backed away. 'You leave me alone,' he shouted. 'Everything I have is mine, you cannot harm me. I have done nothing wrong. I am a man of substance and power in this city, so watch your step.'

No sooner had the young master said this, when Ho Hsien Ku waved a flower in his direction. Suddenly the young man's clothes began to rot on his body. With a horrified cry, he tore them off. Seeing his nakedness, the crowd began to laugh.

When Han Tzu saw how his old master's son had been shamed, he forgot his own sufferings. Pulling off his own jacket, he ran and covered the young man's naked body. The Eight Immortals were greatly moved by this action and ceased tormenting the young master.

Lu Tung Pin looked severely down his nose. 'Young man,' he said, 'it seems you are very foolish. You have one of the world's most honest and wise men in your family and you treat him badly. Now it is your turn to be the servant. For the next seven years, you must serve Han Tzu. At the end of the seven years, we will come to judge you. Be warned. We are severe judges.' So saying, the Immortals disappeared from sight.

After Han Tzuu had recovered from the fright, he led his young master home. For seven years Han Tzu taught the arrogant young man the ways of gentleness and kindness. At first the young man was full of anger and resentment. But over the years he came to see the wise old man as a father.

As they had promised the Eight Immortals returned at the end of seven years. They sent Chang Kuo Lau into the shop to test the young man. He demanded to try on a gold ring. Han Tzu gave it to him, whereupon Chang Kuo Lau threw it to the floor.

'This is rubbish,' he shouted and he spat in Han Tzu's face.

In an instant, the young master jumped to his feet. Snatching up a cloth, he gently wiped the spit from Han Tzu's astonished face. Then he turned to Chang Kuo Lau and said, 'If you are angered, Sir, then spit on me, not on my master.'

With this, Chang Kuo Lau revealed who he really was. When news of the event spread through the streets the whole city came to celebrate the return of the Eight Immortals. But nothing changed in the gold shop. Han Tzu and the young master were now inseparable and they worked side by side for years to come.

When Han Tzu died, the young master wept as if for his own father and he raised a mighty tomb for the wise old man. In turn, he ruled the family with wisdom and gentleness until the time came for him to join his ancestors, becoming a much loved and greatly mourned figure in the city where once he had been so proud and arrogant.

The Dynasties of China

Hsia*	c2000 –	1523 BCE
Shang or Yin*	c1523 –	1028 BCE
Chou*	c1028 –	221 BCE
Early Chou	c1028 –	722 BCE
Ch'un Ch'iu	722 –	480 BCE
Warring States	480 –	221 BCE
Ch'in*	221 –	207 BCE
Han* (Early Han)	207 –	9 CE
Hsin	9 –	23 CE
Han* (Later Han)	23 –	220 CE
Three Kingdoms	220 –	265 CE
Chin		
Western	265 –	317 CE
Eastern	317 –	420 CE
Sung Liu	420 –	479 CE

Separate Northern and Southern Dynasties

Chi.	479 –	502 CE
Liang	502 –	557 CE
Ch'en	557 –	589 CE
Northern Wei	386 –	535 CE
Western Wei	535 –	556 CE
Eastern Wei	534 –	550 CE
Northern Ch'i	550 –	577 CE
Northern Chou	557 –	581 CE

*Major dynasties

Sui*	581	–	618 CE
T'ang*	618	–	907 CE
Five Dynasty Period	907	–	960 CE
Liao (Tartars)	960	–	1125 CE
Hsi Hsia (Tibet)	968	–	1127 CE
Sung*			
Northern	960	–	1127 CE
Southern	1127	–	1279 CE
Chin (Tartar)	1115	–	1234 CE
Yuan* (Mongol)	1260	–	1368 CE
Ming*	1368	–	1644 CE
Ch'ing* (Manchu)	1644	–	1911 CE
Republic	1911	–	1949 CE
People's Republic	1949	–	

*Major dynasties

The Ten Heavenly Stems and the Twelve Earthly Branches

The Ten Heavenly Stems

Stem	Element	Direction
Chia	Wood	East
Yi	Wood	East
Ping	Fire	South
Ting	Fire	South
Wu	Earth	Centre
Chi	Earth	Centre
Keng	Metal	West
Hsin	Metal	West
Jen	Water	North
Kuei	Water	North

The Twelve Earthly Branches

Branch	Animal	Direction
Tzu	Rat	North
Ch'ou	Ox	East
Yin	Tiger	North
Mao	Rabbit	East
Ch'en	Dragon	South
Szu	Snake	East
Wu	Horse	South
Wei	Ram	South
Shen	Monkey	West
Yu	Cock	West
Hsu	Dog	North
Hai	Pig	West

The Chinese Calendar

For Christians BC and AD denote the central historical importance of Jesus. For Moslems, the dates start with Mohemmed's journey to Medina in 622 CE. For Jews, the start of dating time commences with the traditional date of the Creation. For the Chinese, the traditional starting point for reckoning time is 2637 BCE. In this year the Prime Minister of the first of the Five August Emperors, Huang-ti, according to legend, worked out the cycle of 60 years which lies at the centre of calendrical study. For all calendrical study the major problem is the same – how can the solar year be reconciled with the lunar cycle?

The Chinese solution comprises the introduction, every two or three years, of an extra month. The reason for this is quite simple. The lunar year consists of the twelve moons – each moon lasts just over 29½ days. In order to keep the days in each moon as full days, the year is made up of six 'small' months, each being 29 days long and six 'big' months, each being 30 days long. This gives a grand total of 354 days. Occasionally, some years will have seven 'big' months and five 'small' months (a total of 355 days), and some will have seven 'small' months and five 'big' months (a total of 353 days). Thus, on average, each lunar year falls short of the solar year by 10, 11 or occasionally 12 days per year. To bring the calendar in line again, it is necessary to put in an extra month at roughly three-year intervals.

Early on in Chinese astronomy it was noted that over a period of 19 years the sun and moon move through a complete cycle, returning to their relative positions at the end of every 19 years. It seems that this principle was discovered possibly as early as the Shang dynasty. From this, the astronomers were able to evolve regular number of extra months. It was found that during each 19-year cycle, an extra month was needed every seven years.

Apart from the 19-year cycle, the Chinese calendar has the 60-year Sexagenary Cycle. This cycle is of great importance both in fortune telling and recording age. This is shown, for example, in the fact that the only really major celebration of a person's birthday comes when he is 60, for then one complete Sexagenary cycle has been passed through.

The MERIDIAN quality Paperback Collection

(0452)

☐ **THE GERMANS by Gordon A. Craig.** Written by one of the most distinguished historians of modern Germany, this provocative study traces the evolution of the postwar German character by carefully looking at the past and offering a fascinating perspective on German today. (009685—$10.95)

☐ **THE TERRORISM READER: A Historical Anthology edited by Walter Laqueur.** This unique anthology brings together the most notable proponents, critics, and analysts of terrorism from ancient times to today. (008433—$12.95)

☐ **THE GREEK EXPERIENCE by C. M. Bowra.** An extraordinary study of Greek culture, its achievements, and philosophy. With 48 pages of photographs. (009979—$5.95)

☐ **RICE BOWL WOMEN, Writings by and About the Women of China and Japan. Edited, with an introduction and notes, by Dorothy Blair Shimer.** Over a thousand years of stories and memoirs that reflect the changing status and ongoing struggles of women in the Orient. (008271—$4.95)

Prices slightly higher in Canada.

Buy them at your local bookstore or use this convenient coupon for ordering.

NEW AMERICAN LIBRARY
P.O. Box 999, Bergenfield, New Jersey 07621

Please send me the books I have checked above. I am enclosing $_____
(please add $1.00 to this order to cover postage and handling). Send check or money order—no cash or C.O.D.'s. Prices and numbers are subject to change without notice.

Name _____

Address _____

City _____ State _____ Zip Code _____

Allow 4-6 weeks for delivery.
This offer is subject to withdrawal without notice.

MERIDIAN

THE HUMAN MIND

(0452)

☐ **COGNITIVE THERAPY AND THE EMOTIONAL DISORDERS by Aaron Beck, M.D.** In this breakthrough book, Dr. Beck maintains that disordered thinking is at the root of psychological problems, and by showing the patient the ways in which he makes himself a victim with such thinking, most serious mental problems can be overcome. . . . "Immensely readable, logical and coherent . . . this is Beck at his best." —*Psychiatry*   (009286—$8.95)

☐ **GREATNESS AND LIMITATIONS OF FREUD'S THOUGHT by Erich Fromm.** In this, his final book, the world-famous psychoanalyst, social thinker and moral philosopher Erich Fromm presents a lucid appreciation of Freud's work and a keen critique of his failings. "A well-modulated appraisal, and a resonant contribution from the long-popular humanist." —*Kirkus Reviews.*   (009588—$7.95)

☐ **ESSENTIAL PSYCHOTHERAPIES: Theory and Practice by the Masters edited by Daniel Goleman, Ph.D., and Kathleen Riordan, Ph.D.** Beginning with Freud—and including such key figures as Reik, Adler, Reich, Jung, Horney, Sullivan, Bern, Ellis, Perls, Rogers, and May—this anthology brings together the essays in which these thinkers explore the influential new directions they have taken in the treatment of mental illness.   (008840—$7.95)

Prices slightly higher in Canada.